Anti-Bride Etiquette Guide

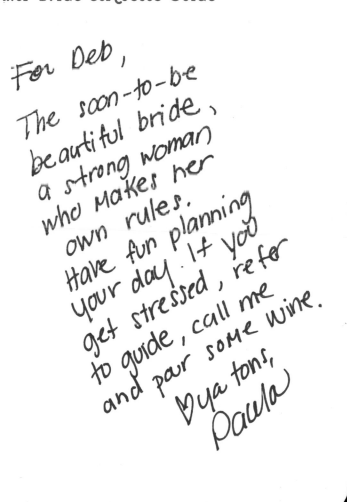

For Deb,
The soon-to-be
beautiful bride,
a strong woman
who makes her
own rules.
Have fun planning
your day. If you
get stressed, refer
to guide, call me
and pour some wine.
♡ya tons,
Paula

Anti-Bride Etiquette Guide
THE RULES—AND HOW TO BEND THEM

by Carolyn Gerin and Kathleen Hughes
Illustrations by Ithinand Tubkam and Carolyn Gerin

CHRONICLE BOOKS
SAN FRANCISCO

For Laurent—best friend, soul mate, and surf instructor. For my late mother. For my grandmother, Dorothy, my inspiration and benchmark for courage and guts. For my father, Barry—the other best guy in my life. For Kathleen, for your perseverance and eagle eye. To Sean, my adored nephew. To Beth, Donnie, Iris, Wyndie—my heart. To Dave and Erin, Don and Jenny, Niall and Jeannie, Rob and Colleen, Iris and John, Darin and Kim—my tribe. To Mikyla Bruder, the girl who turned fantasy into reality and Lisa Campbell for making it happen. To Ithinand Tubkam, my creative soul mate. To Michaela Brockstedt for your nonstop genius and being in my corner. To Alex Rooney, Michael Burns, Michael Thompson, Ashley Fothergill, Gina Catanzaro (fellow gunslinger), Masanori Christianson, Persephone St. Charles, Pete Gowdy, Lisa Mackey, David Lilienstein, David Braun, David Macaione, Jill and Ben Hill and Mary Zencirci, dear friends. To my adored French family, the Gerins—*je vous aime!* To everyone who contributed to this book: Crys Stewart and Litsa Rorris, *Wedding Bells* magazine; Larissa Thompson, *In Style* magazine; Elizabeth Mayhew, *Real Simple* magazine; Peri Wolfman, Williams-Sonoma; Syndie Seid, Advanced Etiquette; Lisa Mackey, Lisa Mackey Design; Lori Leibovitch, Indiebride.com; Wyndie Carter, Bouffant Brides; Peg Devlin Catering; Bridget Brown, Bella Bridesmaids; TwoBrides.com; RainbowWeddingNetwork.com, PrideBride.com; Lisa Holt; Milliken Creek; Lynne Rutter; Lisa Zayas-Chien; Rachel Minard; Danielle MacKinnon; Nickie Amatour; Erin Bell; Michelle Alainiz; Julie Slinger; Stephie Stewart; the Metreon brand goddesses: Eva Miranda, Archie Elwell, Stacey Piket, Heather Hawkins, Rachel Campos, and Judith Klein. To Anti-Brides everywhere who have the guts to challenge the Wedding Industrial Complex. —Carolyn Gerin

Thanks to Nick, my fiancé, who after 7 years, is making an honest woman out of me. I now have the perfect wedding planner to guide me. For Sean, our 5-month old son, who is a complete joy every day of the week. To my family, for always being a huge support network. For Jules, Liz, Dori, Tina, Deena, Katy, and Lizzette—thanks for being my constant sounding board and for being such great friends. And finally, thanks to all of the wedding consultants, caterers, musicians, and, most importantly, brides, who readily gave up their time to talk to us about their experiences. —Kathleen Hughes

Library of Congress Cataloging-in-Publication Data:
Gerin, Carolyn.
 Anti-bride etiquette guide: the rules, and how to bend them / Carolyn Gerin and Kathleen Hughes.
 p. cm.
Includes bibliographical references.
ISBN 0-8118-4458-7
1. Wedding etiquette. 2. Weddings—Planning. I. Hughes, Kathleen. II. Title.

 BJ2051.G4 2004
 395.2'2—dc22

                            2004001702

Manufactured in China.

Designed by Julie Vermeer
Cover illustration by Ithinand Tubkam and Carolyn Gerin

Distributed in Canada by Raincoast Books
9050 Shaughnessy Street
Vancouver, British Columbia V6P 6E5

10   9   8   7   6   5   4   3   2   1

Chronicle Books LLC
85 Second Street
San Francisco, California 94105

www.chroniclebooks.com

CONTENTS

Introduction

Romance! Drama! The wind in your hair, the crash of the ocean, and the ring on your finger! Everything you've ever dreamed of is happening to you—a dress by Vera Wang, catering by Jamie Oliver (who secretly lusts after you), and decorations by Colin Cowie. Your bridesmaids are sleek and chic, smiling in their designer dresses (which are already earmarked for New Year's Eve duty). In your figure-worshiping, custom-designed gown, you've never looked more ravishing. In his Savile Row tux, he's never looked so tall, so handsome. You gaze out at the crowd of your adoring fans: crushed ex-boyfriends, a loving family who get along famously, murderously wealthy in-laws who adore you, and successful and talented friends who are always there for you, no questions asked. You are at the peak of your beauty and this is one of life's most bountiful experiences.

The phone rings. It's your mom, and your father's just told her that you don't want him to walk you down the aisle—you'd rather walk yourself. He's stoic, and she's tearful. It's time for you to snap out of your bridal reverie and back to reality.

The road to your perfect wedding is paved with good intentions. Sometimes that road seems long and winding, and some of the stops you make along the way may leave you feeling awkward and insecure. Did you say the right thing? Did you handle that interaction properly? Why do parents, friends, and even vendors seem to be so sensitive these days? At the root of your uncertainty, you'll often find questions about etiquette. Your wedding, like many hallowed social traditions, comes complete with expectations, rules of conduct, procedures, and prescriptions for behavior. But you're an Anti-Bride, you say, and you don't want that kind of wedding. Well, brava! This is the etiquette book for you.

Your wedding can be the romantic, memorable, and utterly unique event you desire. But first you have to plan it, and planning it will likely get you into more than a few sticky situations. Whether you're choosing your bridesmaids, editing your guest list to fit your smaller-than-expected venue, or taking money from your parents while cringing at their demand that you hire Uncle Bob's polka band, you can't avoid all expectations, traditions, and rules of etiquette. Being an Anti-Bride is about having your wedding your way, without getting bogged down by rules and regulations. But it's also about not offending your loved ones or handling situations in any way that's less than forthright and sensitive. This book will help you identify the rules, understand where other people are coming from, ultimately make the rules work for you, and invent a few rules of your own along the way.

Each chapter, from Chapter 1, The Buck Stops Here, to Chapter 10, The Receiving End—Gifts, starts you off with the Golden Rules, giving you the lowdown on tradition. From there, you'll get guidance on twisting tradition without trauma. Real-life Sticky Situations and stellar solutions help you work out the practical kinks, and useful Stress Savers and Hip Tips keep you sane and stylish. Whether you're worried about navigating the murky waters of announcing your engagement, paring down the guest list, wording your invitation, or selecting friends for your wedding party, the *Anti-Bride Etiquette Guide* will give you the confidence and savvy you need to get it all done with nary a feather ruffled.

At the end of your special day, you'll be filled with the joy of knowing that your wedding brought together the people you love to share in the most amazing event of your life. This book will help you pull it off with style and grace, so that you can have the wedding of your dreams! Read on!

CHAPTER 1

THE BUCK STOPS HERE

We've heard of couples who threw a $50,000 party and then went back to their one-bedroom rental where they wallowed in debt. Or couples who, after asking the question "Who pays?", had to deal with so much family friction that they took off to Vegas. We say that this is no way to begin a life of wedded bliss. Understanding money, the expectations and behaviors attached to it, and the traditional "who pays" scenarios can help you create your own ways-and-means committee that considers your lifestyle, people, and budget.

In this chapter, you'll learn both the traditions and the uncommon twists. You'll get advice on maximizing your outcome, as well as how to build and manage a master budget without burning bridges in the process. In order for your wedding to be stellar, you need to get real. Let's begin with a little history lesson, because, as the saying goes, those who cannot remember the past are doomed to repeat it!

The Golden Rules

Back in the day, it was assumed that the bride's family paid for the primary wedding expenses while the groom's side would handle smaller-ticket items like the rehearsal dinner, marriage license, and honeymoon. These days, it's much more common for the couple and their respective families to share expenses. Still, the old rules do linger and, while the landscape has changed, it's a good idea to know the traditional breakdown of wedding expenses (and who's responsible for them) so you won't be caught off guard if one of your bridesmaids expects you to foot her airfare bill.

Who Pays: THE TRADITION

Bride's Family	Groom's Family
• Invitations, announcements, and other wedding stationery	• Bride's ring (usually purchased and paid for by the groom himself)
• Wedding consultant	• Marriage license and other legal documents
• Location rental for both ceremony and reception	• Gifts for attendants, parents, and bride
• Food and drink	• Officiant's fee
• Musicians	• Bridal bouquet, boutonnieres for best man and groomsmen
• Flower arrangements (not including bouquets for bride and bridesmaids, corsages for mothers, and boutonnieres for groomsmen)	• Attire for parents and groom
• Wedding photography (including their own photo album)	• Travel to the wedding city and lodging for groom's wedding party and close family
• Groom's ring	• Rehearsal dinner
• Gifts for attendants, parents, and groom	• Honeymoon
• Bridesmaid's luncheon	• Groom's family's photo album
• Attire for bride and parents	

Attendants

• Personal attire

• Shower and bachelor/bachelorette party gifts

(Bride's Family continued:)
• Travel to the wedding city and lodging for bride's wedding party and close family

A sharp reader will notice that tradition calls for the bride's family to shell out significantly more money than the groom's side. Why the disparity? The traditional custom was that the bride's family would provide a large dowry to the groom and his family, who would in turn *take the girl (read: liability) off her father's hands.* From the bride's family's perspective, the better the dowry, the better the chance of getting a well-bred, financially stable son-in-law. So isn't it about time we put this nonsense *behind* us? We kicked this sexist and archaic tradition to the curb.

The New Rules of the Road

Hey, we're not here to judge! If your family really wants to pay for the whole wedding, and they are doing it out of love, then break out the bubbly and toast their generosity. But keep in mind that there's no such thing as a free lunch. What may seem like a no-strings-attached gift may in fact come with hidden emotional price tags. Those who don't want to be tied down to tradition, or whose parents simply won't or can't finance a wedding, take heart. There's a new order.

Today, it's commonplace for both families to share in the cost of the wedding festivities, in part because weddings have become so expensive. All this familial love and sharing can make money issues more difficult to sort out, though, mainly because the customary "don't ask, don't tell" approach is replaced by earnest communication (resulting in way more information than people are used to absorbing, especially when it comes to weddings). Who pays these days depends more on who has the ability to pay than on your designated side of the altar. Speaking the truth (with a cherry on top) is the key to success here.

Hip Tip: One savvy bride negotiated deep discounts by renting a ski lodge at Lake Tahoe during the off-season. Cash-strapped guests enjoyed a mini-vacation, complete with scenery, hiking, and clear mountain air, at close to Motel 6 prices!

Time Capsule. Whether the bride was a Rockefeller or born to a family of modest means, in times past etiquette dictated that the wedding would be in the style chosen by the bride's family. If the groom's side did offer to contribute money, they had to tread carefully. Any impression that the contribution was offered in order to alter the bride's family's wedding vision was considered poor manners.

Who Pays: FORGING YOUR OWN PATH

Anti-Brides are all about doing what feels right, which sometimes means bending traditional rules. Here are some strategies for handling the "who pays" dilemma and twisting the tradition without the stress.

THE TWIST	TWISTING WITHOUT TRAUMA
Divide the total bill down the middle—half to the bride's side, and half to the groom's side.	This twist assumes that each side of the family is equally eager to help foot the bill. In this fairly rare case, be sure to develop an accurate budget early on and clearly communicate and agree upon the contributions, and any expectations, before you begin spending.

Hip Tip: Who says a modern girl can't throw in a dash of tradition? Gretchen Hamm, owner of www.TwoBrides.com, a wedding Web site catering to gay, lesbian, bisexual, and transgender couples, says that when planning her daughter's commitment ceremony, both families agreed that the bride's side would pay—so the families split the costs equally.

THE TWIST	TWISTING WITHOUT TRAUMA

Each side of the family pays for their own guests.

This can be a good solution when either family is expecting to invite a lot of people. Chances are that they'll keep their guest list manageable if they're footing the bill. Communication is the key here. You'll need to confirm the guest list very early in the planning stages so that you can secure a location appropriate to the head count. It's also a good idea to figure your budget "per head" (per person), which you can determine by dividing your total budget for the ceremony and reception (see the questionnaire, page 14) by the estimated number of guests. Pass this number on to your respective families, and get them to confirm their proposed head counts.

THE TWIST	TWISTING WITHOUT TRAUMA

The bride and groom pay for everything themselves.

From an Anti-Bride perspective, this is probably the cleanest twist you can take. Paying for your wedding yourself helps ensure that you get your wedding your way. And it's likely that your parents will still want to kick in some money to help out. In that case, graciously accept the money, and make sure you find out if it's intended for something particular; if they're giving you money specifically so you can rent their favorite country club and you plan to get married in the country (sans club), then it's not appropriate to accept the money.

OH, BEHAVE! Don't suggest "stock the wedding bar" or "pass the hat" as a theme for your bridal shower. You should never shake down your guests for wedding costs.

Hopefully you've decided which side of tradition you're on when it comes to who pays, and now it's time to put your money where your mouth is. Knowing your spending limits will curb the money dramas. Use this questionnaire to figure out how much money you have to work with.

1. HOW MUCH MONEY DO WE HAVE? THIS FIGURE SHOULD INCLUDE NOT JUST THE MONEY YOU HAVE TODAY, BUT THE AMOUNT YOU CAN REALISTICALLY SET ASIDE FOR WEDDING EXPENSES BETWEEN NOW AND THE DATE OF YOUR WEDDING.

$ _____

2. ARE WE WILLING TO GO INTO DEBT TO PAY FOR OUR WEDDING? IF SO, WHAT'S OUR DEBT LIMIT? THIS AMOUNT SHOULD BE ONE THAT YOU CAN COMFORTABLY PAY OFF WITHOUT SACRIFICING MORE IMPORTANT GOALS (SUCH AS HOME OWNER-SHIP, OR THE HONEYMOON).

$ _____

3. HOW MUCH IN CONTRIBUTIONS CAN WE COUNT ON FROM OUR LOVED ONES? DON'T ESTIMATE THIS FIGURE! NEVER ASSUME THAT (OR HOW MUCH) YOUR FAMILY WILL CONTRIBUTE. SIT DOWN AND HAVE AN HONEST CONVERSATION WITH THEM, AND MAKE SURE YOU HAVE A CLEAR UNDERSTANDING OF HOW MUCH THEY'RE TRULY HAPPY TO GIVE.

$ _____

Add up the dollar figures from questions 1, 2, and 3. This is your budget. The very word may smack of coupons, meat loaf on Mondays, and spreadsheets, but a budget is an Anti-Bride's best friend. Knowing yours cold will help you make smarter decisions. Sticking to that budget will allow you to have the soiree of your dreams without nose-diving into financial folly.

Sticky Situations

Money is the mother of most sticky situations. Check out these real-life pickles, and our Anti-Bride advice on how to handle these tricky situations.

Your in-laws assume that you're paying for a set of wedding pictures for them.

Solution: First, remember that it's best to let your significant other handle this kind of issue with your in-laws. You're not obligated to pay for a set of pictures for your in-laws or parents, but it is a nice touch to select a few for key people who contributed, either financially or with their time and effort, to the wedding. Circulate the proofs to the family so that they can select and purchase any additional images they really want. Include an order and cost form along with the proofs, plus a handwritten note with any necessary instructions.

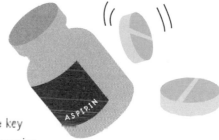

Your parents or in-laws agreed to pay for a portion of the wedding, but the bills are starting to come in at warp speed, and so far, no dough.

Solution: We can't stress enough that the key to managing money issues is clear communication from the beginning about who's paying for what. If you are expecting a certain sum of money or a payment for a specific element of the wedding from your family and it still hasn't come, you will need to ask them directly about the money. If the money is supposed to come from your partner's family, then your partner will need to do the asking. Perhaps they've simply forgotten, they're waiting for a cue from you, or they've had a change of heart. If the latter is the case, you'll need to assess whether you can cover the unexpected costs yourselves and, if not, what you need to sacrifice.

Your partner has called off the wedding. What should you do about the money already spent?

Solution: The person calling off the wedding should cover all nonrefundable expenses (unless, of course, he called it off because he found you in the arms of another). The injured party can claim damages—money paid out in anticipation of the wedding—from the injuring party (who has committed, according to the law, a "breach of promise"). If you've both agreed to call it off, expenses can be split. Any gifts received must be returned, tout de suite.

Some family members who have contributed money want to call the shots.

Solution: Here's why it's important to establish the ground rules before money changes hands. Stephi Stewart, author of *Fire Your Wedding Planner,* says, "Don't wait around for others to take the lead! Stand up for what you want or you'll regret it forever." If your relatives want to help you pay for the wedding, get them to write you a single check for your general wedding fund to use it as you see fit; money allocated for a specific purpose is more likely to have strings attached or come with expectations. If family members aren't comfortable making a general contribution, consider letting them pay for something that isn't a priority item. If you believe the money will come with strings attached, you can decline financial help without ruffling feathers by simply thanking them politely and saying that the financials are covered; then offer them the opportunity to contribute in another area. There's no need to cite their control-freak behavior as a reason for declining the check.

OH, BEHAVE! When you're in need of a few extra bucks for the nuptials, don't cry poverty to your wealthy relatives. Have a heart-to-heart with your parents. And if you find out that they've received unsolicited offers from the aforementioned rich relatives, let them handle the negotiations, and then follow up with a heartfelt thank-you letter.

Your and your intended's families come from very different financial backgrounds, and you're worried about the contribution disparity.

Solution: The financial arrangements should depend on the couple's finances and the family's abilities (and willingness) to cover expenses. Don't advertise one family's contribution in an attempt to influence the other's—you'll only breed insecurities and resentment. If one of your families is struggling financially, don't embarrass them by soliciting contributions. The foolproof strategy for preventing money discomfort is to plan a wedding you can afford yourself. Any money that comes from family can then be considered pennies from heaven.

This is an encore wedding for you or your spouse. How do you ask for money the second time around?

Solution: Traditionally speaking, if the bride's parents paid for the first wedding, they aren't obligated to pay for the second. But it really boils down to the individuals involved—some parents wouldn't hear of their daughter paying for her own wedding and would offer to contribute money (even if she's been married before), while others would need to be approached. If your parents don't offer money spontaneously, it's your call whether to dare to ask. Just be prepared to respect the answer. Our advice? Lose your expectations, forget your desired results, and work with what you have.

CHAPTER 2

RULES OF ENGAGEMENT

Being the discriminating and discerning gal that you are, you've probably said "I don't" far more often in your lifetime than "I do." And though you've never been one to wait around for anything (or anyone), that special someone has found his or her way into your life and the inevitable has happened: *you're engaged.*

After your head stops spinning, you'll find yourself bursting with questions: Whom do I tell first? What's expected of me? What do I do next? In this chapter we'll take you through the practicalities of your engagement—from the ring to the big announcement. You'll find out the traditional—and the Anti-Bride—ways of spreading the happy news without offending anyone or making yourself crazy, and some strategies to get the engagement ring you want (hint: diamonds are overrated!).

The Golden Rules

The whole idea of an engagement is in itself pretty old-fashioned. It's not surprising, then, that becoming engaged and announcing the engagement involve plenty of traditions.

Announcing Your Engagement: THE TRADITION

Although they may strike you as constricting—you may feel like picking up the phone and calling your best friend before you tell anyone else—the old-fashioned rules about whom to tell first are actually well intentioned: think of how your mother would feel if she knew she wasn't the first person you came to with the news. The traditional order in which to inform your loved ones is as follows: nearest and dearest family members (the bride's family first, followed by the groom's), then extended family, and finally friends and co-workers. Of course, if you're a by-the-book gal, then your parents already know you're tying the knot—because your intended asked your dad for his permission before proposing.

Traditionally, soon after the bride and groom have announced their engagement to their close friends and relatives, each family hosts a small celebration in honor of the couple: dinner at a local restaurant, an informal cocktail party, or anything in between. Then, some time thereafter, there's the engagement party, where the "formal" announcement is made, usually by the bride's father. The bride's parents usually host this fete, which includes family and friends who will be invited to the nuptials.

Time Capsule. In previous decades, it was considered proper to send a handwritten or printed engagement announcement to friends and family members not attending the engagement party.

After the couple declares their intentions to family and friends, the next step (a lovely old-world concept) is to announce the engagement to the community. Many newspapers publish a weekly page announcing local couples' engagements, weddings, and anniversaries. A conventional newspaper announcement contains personal information including the couple's names, date and general location of the wedding, cities of residence, parents' names, occupations, schooling, and other notable accomplishments. Many couples choose to include a photo of themselves as well. Below is an example of a traditional newspaper announcement.

> MR. AND MRS. RON SMITH OF SAN FRANCISCO, CALIFORNIA, ANNOUNCE THE ENGAGEMENT OF THEIR DAUGHTER RUBY TO CHRISTOPHER REESE, THE SON OF MR. AND MRS. ROBERT REESE OF SEATTLE, WASHINGTON. THE WEDDING WILL TAKE PLACE IN OCTOBER 2005. MISS SMITH IS A GRADUATE OF THE XYZ COLLEGE AND WORKS AS A LIBRARIAN FOR ABC CORPORATION. MR. REESE IS A GRADUATE OF UNIVERSITY OF XYZ AND WORKS AS A TECHNICIAN FOR DEF & COMPANY.

Time Capsule. In the 1800s, well-off couples were usually engaged for only a few months. Since vendors weren't booked a year or more in advance, as they are now, and elaborate parties were commonplace, there wasn't any reason to wait.

New Rules of the Road

An engagement is a highly personal, yet oddly public, stage in one's relationship. There are lots of expectations and traditions that certain brides follow, but since you're an Anti-Bride, feel free to write your own ticket!

Announcing Your Engagement: FORGING YOUR OWN PATH

After the proposal, you may want to shout your news from the rooftops, or you might prefer to savor the pleasure privately for a few months before you alert the media. There's no law that says you must follow the rules. If you'd prefer not to adhere to a particular tradition but you're having trouble deciding whom to tell first, use the following rule of thumb: To avoid causing injured feelings, start with the people who are closest to you, and work from there. Sending your engagement announcement to your local newspaper before you've finished telling your closest family members and friends would be a fatal faux pas.

We love the idea of the engagement party—any excuse to raise a glass with our favorite people is good enough for us! But etiquette doesn't require you to hold it in prix fixe restaurantland. Why not throw an outdoor luau, complete with slack-key guitar music, a roast pig, and tropical cocktails? If you're hosting your own wedding, or if your parents aren't hung up on the "proper" way of doing things, you may also twist tradition by having your best friend, your grandmother, or your favorite teacher make the official announcement at the soiree. *For more alternative engagement party ideas, see chapter 7.*

Does your intended's mother want you to go the conventional route and publish your engagement news in the local paper? Imagine this: here's your chance to get the attention of all those exes who didn't have the good sense to appreciate a good thing when they had it. Go ahead and brag a little! If you decide to send in a photo of yourselves with the announcement, you'll probably want to choose one that is classy and tasteful; deep cleavage, heavy petting, and cocktails in hand (unless it's the clinking of champagne glasses) do not enhance engagement photos.

But what if your family (or your romance) isn't exactly conventional—for example, your parents are divorced, both have remarried, and all four spouses want to be mentioned in the announcement? Below are sample newspaper announcements you can adapt to fit your situation. If you're a same-sex couple, keep in mind that many newspapers are now listing upcoming commitment ceremonies right up there with the society girls' announcements.

Divorced parents: Ms. Grace Smith of San Francisco, California, and Mr. Ron Smith of San Francisco, California, announce the engagement of their daughter Ruby to Christopher Reese of Seattle, Washington, son of . . .

Remarried parent(s): Mr. and Mrs. Ron Smith of San Francisco, California, announce the engagement of Mr. Smith's daughter Ruby to Christopher Reese. Miss Smith is also the daughter of Grace Anderson of Silver Spring, Maryland, who is married to Mr. Frederick Anderson. Mr. Reese is the son of . . .

Deceased parent: Mr. and Mrs. Ron Smith of San Francisco, California, announce the engagement of Mr. Smith's daughter Ruby to Christopher Reese of Seattle, Washington. Miss Smith is also the daughter of the late Grace Smith. Mr. Reese is the son of . . .

Couple announces: The engagement of Ruby Smith and Christopher Reese of Seattle, Washington, has been announced. Miss Smith is the daughter of Ron and Grace Smith of San Francisco, California. Mr. Reese is the son of . . .

RING TRUE

The white-gold setting with the requisite diamond is so passé, but many guys (and gals) think going down any other path is heresy. Lisa Mackey, jewelry pro, says that brides should strut their signature style. Thick, heavy settings with big, bright-colored stones like canary or pink diamonds, rubies, and emeralds are perfectly appropriate. As long as you love your ring and it expresses your personality and fashion sense, why follow the pack with a boring white diamond?

For something different, try going vintage. Browse your favorite antique shops for rings from the 1930s and 1940s, when intricate settings and gorgeous stone colors were in vogue. Or mark your territory in permanent ink. For the jewelry challenged, nothing says "I do" quite like matching tattoos on the bride's and groom's ring fingers. Finally, there's no rule that says you must have an engagement ring *and* a wedding band. If your engagement ring is beautiful just the way it is, don't feel pressured to pair it with a wedding band. Or, if you prefer things simple, skip the engagement ring altogether.

Time Capsule. The diamond, first set in engagement rings in medieval Italy, was chosen to stand for enduring love because of its hardness and durability.

Stress Saver. Picking a romantic destination to pop the big question is fabulous, but make sure your travel insurance covers the ring. Or be investment savvy and wedding wise: use a "placeholder" ring until you return home. That way you can go swimming, and lose the hassle of using the hotel safe.

Sticky Situations

Getting engaged and announcing an engagement can involve plenty of sticky situations, especially with regard to that all-important symbol, the engagement ring. Take a look at these predicaments and their possible solutions.

One of you has called off the engagement.

Solution: If you're the one who has broken it off, then you must return the engagement ring and all gifts your fiancé gave you. If your fiancé is the one who has backed out, then you may legally keep the engagement ring and any gifts he has given you. (Some brides return the ring anyway, especially if it's a family heirloom.)

Regardless of who has called it off, any wedding gifts you've received should be returned with a note that says, "I'm sorry to inform you that Bob and I have broken off our engagement. With my regrets, I am returning your generous gift." If you've already sent out wedding invitations you can get the news out via short handwritten notes, or by telephone. Keep in mind that informing guests by telephone will automatically put you in explanation mode. You don't need to share the gory details with everyone. If they press you for information, tell them you've got numerous calls to make, and that you'll download at a later date.

Your parents detest your fiancé.

Solution: First, ask your parents why they disapprove, and then sit back and really listen to their response (assume that deep down your parents love you and want what's best for you). Once they've aired their concerns, explain your position: the reasons you love this person are x, y, and z, and you are standing by your decision to spend the rest of your life with him or her. Let them know that it would mean a lot to you if they accepted your partner. If they refuse, tell yourself that life ain't fair, and that to follow your heart is the noblest thing you can do in life.

You hate your engagement ring.

Solution: If there is any redeeming quality to the ring (the luminous stone or the platinum setting, for example), focus on that first. But if you just can't bring yourself to adore it, then soon after he gives it to you explain what you like about the ring and tell him that you'd like to pay a jeweler to change it to suit your style. If you just can't stand the ring, period, sit down with him and tell him that you love the gesture *(and him)*, but you want to exchange it for another ring. Make sure he knows that you'll pay the difference if the new ring costs more. Stress that you want to have a ring that you love as much as you love him, since you will be wearing it every day for the rest of your life. Explain that you want your ring to remind you of how much you love him every time you look at it. Don't wait too long to tell him—you'll only have a few weeks to return it.

Your partner's family is pressuring you to wear an heirloom ring you loathe.

Solution: Honesty is the best policy, since your engagement ring will be an integral part of your daily life for a long time. Tell your fiancé that you already have an idea of the ring you want and that, while you're crazy in love with him, you're not crazy about his family's ring. Do let him know if you're open to using the heirloom ring's gem in another setting. If it's a money issue (i.e., your intended doesn't have much of it), you may have to kick in some funds to make your dream ring happen. You'll be in good company—many brides do this in order to ensure that they have a ring they love.

OH, BEHAVE! "Recycling" an engagement ring is fine. An heirloom (as long as the bride likes it) can be gorgeous. But don't reuse a ring from a previous marriage or engagement—it's tacky (and a bit of a bad omen).

Your fiancé wants to pick out and pay for your ring, but you have very different tastes and the ring you want is well beyond his price range.

Solution: Whether it's the size of the rock or the design of the setting you're concerned about, you'll need to be clear what your expectations are. Gently guide him (by showing him examples in magazine ads or store windows) toward styles you like. Be realistic: if he can only afford a modest ring, don't expect him to go broke buying you a Liz Taylor museum piece—instead, offer to pay the difference (any other course of action smacks of "gold digger"). If he insists on picking it out, make sure he knows your taste. He may choose a smaller stone, but we'd bet our tiaras that down the road, when he's doing better financially, you won't want to trade up.

Your partner "let the cat out of the bag" about your engagement before you were ready to go public.

Solution: The first thing you need to do is find out exactly whom he told (read: damage control). Just his parents or his siblings? If so, ask your fiancé to swear them to secrecy until you've had a chance to make the announcement to your own family. If he has set the rumor mill in motion, you'll need to move quickly so your family members don't hear about it from some well-meaning acquaintance they run into in the supermarket. Call your own family members and then your close friends with the news, make arrangements to send written announcements to other friends and acquaintances, and then get the newspaper announcement together. If your feelings have been hurt by your partner's indiscretion, tell him how you feel. You want to start your beautiful life together with honesty, not mistrust.

CHAPTER 3

THE GUEST LIST

When deciding on your guest list, approach the task as you would a real-estate purchase: with a cold eye and an appreciation of the bottom line. You have a limited amount of money and space. You know the people you want to invite (your tribe), as well as the people you feel you should invite. Your job is to figure out how to edit the list without experiencing emotional blackmail or fiscal folly.

Utilizing discretion and tact will keep you above the fray in this tension-fraught game known as Creating the Wedding Guest List. This chapter will help you pare it down, deal with the "plus ones," arrange appropriate lodging for your out-of-town guests, and manage a myriad of other etiquette issues.

The Golden Rules

The Guest List: THE TRADITION

The way you slice and dice the guest list has never been set in stone, but often those holding the purse strings have quite a lot of say. Generally speaking, guest lists are divided in half between families, or into thirds—one-third for each family, and one-third for the couple. Some circumstances warrant that the scales be tipped a bit, if one family is significantly larger or the wedding is being held in the bride's or groom's hometown, for example.

New Rules of the Road

The Guest List: FORGING YOUR OWN PATH

Because you, like all Anti-Brides (and their grooms), want to create a meaningful event that includes the key people in your life, compiling the guest list isn't as agonizing as it may seem. Isn't your wedding day all about being surrounded by people who care about *you?* Instead of going the old-fashioned route and dividing the guest slots according to who's paying, use our sure-fire way to assemble your best people and preserve the love. Ask yourself, If I had to build a community to live with on an otherwise uninhabited island, whom would I choose? Start there, and then make allowances for your parents' guests, adding or subtracting as you go along. Some people will be casualties, while others will make the cut (especially if they've contributed time or money to your wedding cause). Follow the steps listed here for stress-free, fat-free guest-list decision making:

> **Hip Tip.** Let the fire marshal be the heavy. Citing your venue's strict observance of capacity limits is a good way to avoid being seen as the bad apple by extended family members. Say, "I'm so sorry. I wish we could include you, but the place only holds a limited number of people, and by law we can't exceed that number."

1. **Identify the number of people you would like to have at your wedding.** If you've already decided on your budget and the location for the event, this number will probably be determined by space limitations or the cost per head.

2. **Compile your master list first.** First, grab some paper and pencils and sit down with your fiancé. Each of you should write down the names of the people you think should be on the guest list, separated into A, B, and C lists. The A list includes people who *must* be there: closest friends and family; the B list is composed of people you *want* to be there: favorite co-workers and more distant friends and family; the C list includes people you'd *like* to be there: your local bartender, long-lost relatives, and cubicle comrades.

3. **Combine your lists with your fiancé's.** Do this on a computer, paper, or index cards. Then tally up the A-list people. These people are nonnegotiable. Tally up the B and C lists to come up with a grand total. Compare this number with the figure from item 1, above. If you've exceeded your ideal number of guests, see if you can eliminate anyone (or consider renting a larger facility, if you haven't already booked one). If you still have slots to fill, move on to item 4.

4. **Give the lists to your parents and have them review and add their own A, B, and C people.** Their must-have lists will come second to yours. Stand your ground on the total number of people they can add, but be considerate—if your mom has her heart set on her favorite cousin being there, then invite her.

Regardless of how you slice the pie, our advice is to always maintain control. If nothing else, remember that, when all the names are compiled, you have the final word on the list, including children and plus-ones.

Stress Saver. One bride suggests following up on *all* RSVPs two weeks before the wedding. In her case, several people who had written her that they were coming never showed up. If they'd let her know ahead of time, she could have invited some of her B-list people she had been forced to exclude. **Note:** Not showing up to a wedding post-RSVP guarantees expulsion from the couple's A list in the future.

Sticky Situation

If money and space are not an issue, consider yourself one of the lucky few, and invite with abandon. But if you're not that fortunate, you're bound to run into some etiquette dilemmas as you first create and then pare down your guest list. Here are a few common sticky situations and our views on how to get unstuck.

Your cousin asks if you're inviting her college-age daughter—in said daughter's presence.

Solution: What to do? Should you bite the bullet and add another guest to your list (opening a cousinly can of worms that's sure to explode as the news spreads), or do you tell it like it is? If you want to keep the peace with your cousin *and* the other one hundred family

---

GUEST EXPECTATIONS, PART I

Knowing what makes a good guest can help guide you if you're faced with unseemly guest behavior before the wedding. Good guests do the following:

- *They reply to the invitation quickly and send a gift within one year after the wedding. (Although you shouldn't expect a gift, chances are that you'll be getting one.) Guests who don't attend are not required to send a gift.*

- *They ask the appropriate registry questions. Brides aren't expected to spontaneously volunteer the names of the stores where they've registered. Guests are expected to take the initiative to ask for registry information. It's fine to ask the bride, her mother, or the maid of honor about the particulars.*

- *They mail the gift instead of schlepping it to the soiree. The bride and groom shouldn't perform sherpa duty (transport a carload of boxes to their home the night before they fly to Paris), especially if the goal is to enjoy a proper wedding night.*

GOLD DIGGER (FINDING THE BEST DIGS FOR OUT-OF-TOWNERS)

Your guests will be groped by airport security, crammed into tiny airplane seats, and living out of suitcases, just for the privilege of witnessing your nuptials. Show your appreciation by identifying and even arranging extra-special overnight accommodations for out-of-town guests. Yes, they could do this themselves, but it's thoughtful (and, frankly, expected) for you to do some legwork for them in advance.

- *If your wedding's at a hotel, start there for convenience and a possible discount. If you're getting hitched elsewhere, check out local chains, B&Bs, and inns in the area. Try to select hotels within two miles of the festivities—the closer the better.*

- *Since guests pay for their own rooms, keep their financial situations in mind. Your grad school pals may want something modest while your older relatives may prefer cushy amenities—pick a variety of hotels and let them choose.*

- *Reserve blocks of rooms at the hotels you've chosen, and ask for a group discount—guests can then make their own reservations, but they'll appreciate the discount and the time you've saved them.*

- *Put together a fact sheet or e-mail blast containing details on local car rental companies, local restaurants, museums, and hot spots. You can mail them the fact sheet ahead of time or include it in a goody bag you'll present to them when they arrive.*

members who would surely blackball you for not also inviting their kids, use this script: "Although I would love to include all of my cousins, I know that if I invite one, I must out of fairness invite all. Unfortunately, our venue and our budget can't handle another person." If you're less than two weeks away from your wedding day, you might add, "And my final count is now with the caterer."

You want to advance your career without inviting everyone in your office.

Solution: It's a wedding, not a pool party. This is a dignified, once-in-a-lifetime event—do you really want re-create the office dynamic at your nuptials? Just invite your *best* pals (and maybe your boss) from the office, mailing their invitations to their homes. Send the B-list people, like the company's CEO (assuming you don't work directly with him or her), invitations only if there are slots available. Your co-workers will understand if you don't invite them, just as long as you don't talk about your wedding plans incessantly or spend hours on the phone or Web making wedding plans on the company's dime.

Your mother has been telling her Pilates classmates and all of her neighbors that they'll be invited to your wedding, and she seems to have no intention of stopping.

Solution: Since nobody's actually been invited, there's really nobody to uninvite. Immediately muzzle your mom, nicely. Using your sweetest, most understanding tone, ask her not to invite anyone without clearing it with you first. Explain that unless a guest gets a written invitation, they won't be attending, and you won't send a written invitation unless she checks with you first. Remind her that your venue only holds a certain amount of people, and that your budget's not unlimited. If your mother is worried about her friends' reactions, tell her that most people understand that a casual "ya'll come on down" doesn't hold a lot of water. When the date comes and goes, they'll realize that they didn't make the cut, and your mother will have to explain herself, if asked. She probably won't be asked.

Hip Tip. For a destination wedding (or if you'll be inviting a lot of out-of-towners), send save-the-date cards at least three or four months in advance. Helping guests save on travel costs is a divinely thoughtful gesture.

You want to keep it small, but your in-laws have different ideas.

Solution: Talk to your partner first. If you decide on a firm fifty guests, you need to present a united front. Sit down with both sets of parents and relay that message. Offer to cohost a post-wedding party where they can invite business associates and others who didn't attend the wedding itself. Repeat this Anti-Bride mantra to yourself: "It's our day, not our parents' day." Hold on to your vision.

You're having a small wedding, and a guest calls you to ask if she can bring her new beau, a guy she met in a nightclub three days ago.

Solution: Set up criteria excluding everyone but friends, family members, and their *truly* significant others. Say, "I'm so happy that you've met someone you like, and we're thrilled that you'll be sharing our day with us, but this is such an intimate and personal occasion in our lives. We'll be so much more comfortable celebrating with people we know and love, instead of someone we've never met." Be kind, firm, and authoritative.

A friendly acquaintance assumes she's invited but she's not.

Solution: If it's early and you haven't made any big decisions on budget and head count, warn the assuming acquaintance that your budget may be limited, which may mean a smaller wedding. This way, she won't be surprised when she's not on the list. If she's heard about your three-hundred-person soiree, you'll have to make a judgment call. If you decide to leave her off the guest list, it could be a relationship ender. Our advice? Call some of your A-list people you think might not come and gently find out their intentions. If you end up with an open slot, bump her up to first class.

Two weeks before your wedding, a friendly acquaintance, assuming that her invitation must have gotten delayed in the mail, mentions that she hasn't received one.

Solution: Be frank but apologetic, saying, "Actually, our small budget really limited the number of people we could invite. I wish we could have included you, but unfortunately it wasn't possible." However, if you'd really like to invite this person, see how many RSVPs you've received (before you give the final head count to your caterer); if you have room, call her and invite her.

You receive RSVP cards from guests who have added on uninvited people.

Solution: Inviting guests to someone else's wedding is beyond brash. Call up the original invitees and tell them how happy you are that they're coming but that, unfortunately, you can't accommodate anyone other than those on your guest list. The offending guest might offer to pay for the extra dinner, but we say it's your wedding, not a hot restaurant where you can buy off the maître d'. Cite maximum-occupancy restrictions, or speak your mind, saying that you've invited only your very nearest and dearest and you'd like their help with upholding your vision. If they can't attend without their entourage, gently help them to realize that it's your wedding and the velvet rope starts with you.

You didn't include some shower guests on your wedding list.

Solution: For shame! By law all shower attendees must receive an invite. Immediately include them on the A list, and send them an invitation right away.

Hip Tip. If you're having a destination wedding or an intimate family-only wedding, hold a celebration after your honeymoon and invite everyone who either didn't come or wasn't invited to the wedding, to smooth any ruffled feathers.

You know that some of the guests on your list won't be able to attend.

Solution: Whether or not the person can attend, he or she will appreciate being included. In fact, if you don't send an invitation to a close friend or relative, she may feel slighted, even if she will be out of town. If you fear that she may think you're fishing for gifts, don't worry—gifting is the guest's call, not yours.

Your fiancé doesn't want your ex at the wedding.

Solution: Take the cue from your intended. Anyone who vibes your mate out on your wedding day shouldn't be at your wedding. Even if you're friends with your ex, there are no romantic feelings between you whatsoever, and he is a member in good standing with your tribe, you must indulge your fiancé's whims, however obsessive they may seem. Do not apologize for your fiancé's feelings or rationalize this decision to others—he has a right to feel uncomfortable around your old flame. If your ex truly cares about you, he will gracefully bow out. Stand shoulder to shoulder with your fiancé regarding your decision, and go forward guilt free.

Family members are uncomfortable with the same-sex ceremony you're planning and you think their presence at the wedding might create tension.

Solution: According to Gretchen Hamm of www.TwoBrides.com, the best approach for dealing with a family member who isn't on board with your lifestyle is to give them an easy out. Whether it's an advocate (mom or sibling) who speaks to the relative on your behalf, or a wedding location only the closest pals and relatives would travel to, the idea is to let them off the hook gracefully. Whatever the situation, you need to respect the feelings of those who love you and try to understand if they're not ready to accept some of your life choices. As a result, they won't feel as if they have offended you, and you'll have a much more Zen-like attitude knowing that everyone at your celebration is behind you 100 percent. The upside? You won't have to skulk at opposite ends of the living room at Thanksgiving.

CHAPTER 4

INVITATIONS & STATIONERY

A wedding invitation does more than provide the 411 on your event. It also offers a hint of what's in store for your guests—a swank black-tie soiree, a tropical destination luau, or a Gatsby-esque garden party. Since you may not have experience hosting a party requiring anything more elaborate than an Evite, you'll want to pay close attention to the P's and Q's of getting the word out.

Designing, creating, and ordering invitations can be overwhelming. Tallying the guest list, assembling myriad pieces comprising the invitation (reply cards, admission cards, entrée-choice cards, interior envelopes, and those little pieces of mystery tissue), and assembling them can flummox even the socially savvy. This chapter will introduce you to all of the things that make up an invitation, including the rules of etiquette. When addressing an invitation to your aunt who is in the process of a divorce and a name change but has a live-in, same-sex significant other, you'll know exactly what to do. You'll learn how to assemble formal and informal invitations, and how to be erudite yet concise in all wedding-related missives, all the while maintaining your good manners and your inimitable Anti-Bride style.

The Golden Rules

Wedding and invitation styles go hand in hand. Generally, the more formal the wedding, the fancier the invitation.

The Invitation: THE TRADITION

Formal invitations are engraved with black, brown, or gray ink on weighty white or off-white stock. Reception information is engraved on a separate card, in the matching typeface and paper. Both the invitation and the reception card are placed, with any enclosures, in an inner unsealed envelope, which is then inserted in an outer envelope. Both envelopes are addressed by hand. For formal invitations, information sheets containing hotel accommodations and directions should be mailed separately, although many user-friendly brides will send this information all together.

For informal invitations, artistic expression, photography, and computer-generated designs are appropriate options. Paper color and font selection should reflect the personality of the couple and event. Maps and hotel information, printed on the same paper stock and typeface of the invitation, are usually mailed with the invitation. If you have a time crunch (i.e., the wedding is less than a month away) and your wedding is ultra informal, you can send handwritten notes or e-mail messages and guests may respond by phone or e-mail.

Time Capsule. Beginning in the eighteenth century, when invitations were hand delivered, the outer envelope was used to keep the invitation envelope clean for a more impressive presentation. Today, most formal invitations include outer and inner envelopes while informal invitations don't.

Stress Saver. Order invitations four to six months in advance, and mail them six to eight weeks before the wedding. You'll probably get a few returned in the mail that you'll have to resend.

PRINTING THAT FITS THE EVENT

TYPE	DESCRIPTION	BEST FOR...	COST
Engraving	Paper is stamped with a die, leaving an imprint, and then ink is applied. Produces raised print on the front and depression on the back.	Formal to very formal weddings	Most expensive
Thermography	A heat process that fuses ink and powder. Looks like engraving but letters are raised only in the front.	Informal to semi-formal	Less expensive than engraving
Lithography	Creates watercolor effects and pale background designs. The ink is literally flat with a matte finish.	Informal to semi-formal	Less expensive than thermography
Printed	Can be produced in a print shop or at home. May require using lighter-weight stock to get paper through printer.	Informal	Cheapest

 OH, BEHAVE! For formal invitations, when referring to the half hour, "half after two o'clock" is considered proper, while "two thirty" is not.

INVITATION DOS AND DON'TS

Do	Don't
. . . send formal paper invitations and handwritten thank-you notes.	. . . e-mail your wedding invitations (unless your wedding is very informal and less than a month away) or thank-you notes.
. . . allow the family grapevine to spread the word about your gift registry.	. . . include information concerning your gift registry in your wedding invitations. An invitation is simply a request for someone's presence at your event, not a request for gifts.
. . . send separate invitations to adult family members (eighteen years or older) living under the same roof. For small children, see the discussion on addressing invitations on page 49.	. . . address an invitation to "Mr. William Jones and family."

FINDING THE WORDS

Finding the appropriate words for invitations can stump the best of us. Etiquette suggests the following: the more formal the wedding, the more traditional the wording. Below, you'll find some examples of invitation wordsmithing.

FORMAL

Bride's family hosts:

Mr. and Mrs. Ron Smith
request the honor of your presence
at the marriage of their daughter
Ruby Ann
to
Christopher John Reese

on Saturday, the sixth of June
two thousand and four
at three o'clock

Saint Paul's Church
San Francisco, California

(The reception invitation is printed as a separate card and included with the ceremony invitation.)

INFORMAL

Bride's family hosts:

The Smith Family
invites you to celebrate the love of
Ruby Ann
and
Christopher John Reese

on their wedding day
June 6, 2004

at 3:00 P.M.

Saint Paul's Church
San Francisco, California

Reception to follow
Butterfly Restaurant

FORMAL

Groom's family hosts:

Mr. and Mrs. Robert Reese

request the honor of your presence
at the marriage of

Ruby Ann Smith
to their son
Christopher John . . .

INFORMAL

Groom's family hosts:

The Reese Family

invites you to witness the marriage of

Ruby Ann Smith
to their son
Christopher John . . .

FORMAL

Couple hosts:

Ruby Ann Smith
and
Christopher John Reese

request the honor of your presence
at their marriage . . .

INFORMAL

Couple hosts:

Ruby Smith and Chris Reese

are beginning the adventure of a lifetime

Please join them as they say their
vows of marriage . . .

FORMAL

Both families host:

Mr. and Mrs. Ron Smith
and
Mr. and Mrs. Robert Reese

request the honor of your presence
at the marriage of their children

Ruby Ann
and
Christopher John . . .

INFORMAL

Both families host:

The Smith and Reese families
invite you to share their joy
as their children

Ruby Ann
and
Christopher John

are united in marriage . . .

FORMAL

Divorced parents cohost:

Mrs. Grace Jones
and
Mr. Ron Smith

request the honor of your presence
at the marriage of their daughter

Ruby Ann
to
Christopher John Reese . . .

INFORMAL

Divorced parents cohost:

Grace Jones and Ron Smith

invite you to celebrate the marriage
of their daughter

Ruby Ann
to
Christopher John Reese . . .

RECEPTION INVITATION

Inviting some guests to the reception but not the ceremony is considered acceptable. To do this, simply send those guests an invitation to the reception (which does not mention the ceremony) only. For those guests you'd like to also invite to the ceremony, order a small card in exactly the same color, paper stock, and printing method as those used for the wedding invitation, providing the details. Include the reception card in the invitation envelope.

FORMAL

Typical reception invitation wording for a formal wedding (if the bride's parents are hosting), to be printed as a separate card:

Mr. and Mrs. John Smith

request the pleasure of your company

Saturday, the sixth of June
two thousand and four
at four o'clock

XYZ Country Club

R.S.V.P.
1425 ABC Street
San Francisco

INFORMAL

Typical wording for an informal wedding, to be included on the ceremony invitation card:

Reception immediately following the ceremony

XYZ Country Club
200 JKL Avenue
San Francisco

R.S.V.P.
1425 ABC Street
San Francisco

OH, BEHAVE!

When you're compiling your guest list and addressing your invitations, don't do the "and guest" routine. On your list, put a checkmark next to the names of people you think may have a significant other and call them to find out. If the answer is yes, put that person's name on the invitation.

Real Simple magazine's Elizabeth Mayhew says using computer-generated addresses is fine for very informal events, but invitations for large, formal weddings should be addressed by hand. The logic? Mass mailings lack that personal touch. And, since hotel chains in Maui use computer-generated addresses on heavy, expensive envelopes when sending promotional mailers, your guests might think your invite is yet another high-end travel promo and toss it.

Stress Saver. Assign each invitation recipient a number, and lightly write that number in pencil on the back of that person's reply card. Keep a list of these numbers and their corresponding names. Then, when your guests send in their reply cards and you can't read someone's handwriting, you can use your code to determine the mystery guest's identity, saving face all around.

WEDDING STATIONERY

Need a primer on the many wedding stationery products? Wondering what all those pieces floating around in that envelope are? Here's a glossary of those mysterious items you might find in an invitation or on the stationery company's order form.

Admission card: Guests present this to the attendant bouncers at the door to let them know they're in the club. If you think your crazy ex might try to crash your event, admission cards will keep the ceremony gated.

At-home card: This provides the couple's new address to their friends and family members. They can be sent with wedding announcements or invitations, or one can be discreetly displayed at the wedding reception. Below is an example of proper wording:

Mr. and Mrs. Christopher Reese

after June sixth

1011 Easy Street
San Francisco, California
415.444.4444

Entree choice card: This card, mailed with the invitation, allows guests to preselect an entree (if more than one is offered). We think this is more airline than wedding.

Map and direction sheet: This sheet provides the ceremony and reception sites' street addresses and directions. They may be mailed with informal invitations, or separately if the wedding is formal.

Menu: This elegant card, traditionally used for a formal, sit-down dinner and displayed at the reception, lists the dishes to be served at each course.

Personal stationery: You can order note cards in the style of your wedding invitations for writing thank-you notes before and after the wedding. Any notes written before the wedding should be signed with your maiden name.

Pew card: This card is meant to reserve particular seats for family members at the ceremony. They should be printed or engraved with the guest's name, and the pew number handwritten on the card. These cards are often mailed with the invitation. If the bride would rather wait until RSVPs have been received, she can then send handwritten pew cards to those who will be attending the wedding. Pew numbers are generally handwritten on the card.

> **Example:**   PEW NUMBER 5
>
> MR. AND MRS. RON REESE

Place cards and table numbers: These are used to reserve particular seats for guests at the reception. Table numbers are positioned in a visible spot on the tables, and place cards with corresponding table numbers are usually laid out on a table near the entrance to the reception. Names and numbers should be handwritten on cards that echo the style of your wedding invitations.

Reply card: Guests use these to indicate whether or not they'll be attending the wedding. Those with a little blue blood flowing in their veins won't need a reply card (they know that to send a handwritten note on their own stationery is the utmost in propriety), but most guests aren't aware of that etiquette custom and find it convenient to reply if a preprinted card and preaddressed, stamped envelope are provided. Some cards are preprinted for convenience (see below), while others also offer blank space inside for guests to write a note to the couple, who may keep especially meaningful notes as keepsakes.

> **Here is the typical wording:**
>
> *The favor of your reply is requested by xyz date.*
>
> *M_____ _____ _____*
>
> *Accepts__*
>
> *Regrets__*

Save-the-date cards: Sending these is a must for a destination wedding and advisable if you're inviting out-of-town guests. They should be mailed four to six months in advance and don't require a reply. For less formal weddings, they can take the form of a simple postcard or handwritten note.

Tissue: In the past, sheets of tissue were placed over the invitation to prevent the ink from smudging. With modern printing methods, this practice is no longer necessary, but some traditions, like this one, just won't die.

Wedding announcement: Couples send these after the ceremony to those who were not invited to attend the wedding and reception. An at-home card is customarily included as well.

Traditional wording for a formal wedding:

Mr. and Mrs. Ron Smith

have the honor of announcing
the marriage of their daughter

Ruby Ann
to
Christopher John Reese

on Saturday, the sixth of June
two thousand and four

Saint Paul's Church
San Francisco

Wedding program: The program, handed out to guests as they arrive at the ceremony site, lists the order of the service; any readings, poems, or songs read or played during the ceremony; and the names of the wedding party members, readers, and performers.

Within the ribbons card: Used at large, formal weddings, this small printed card, mailed with the invitation, is presented by guests to the usher to let him know that they should be seated in a special section.

Hip Tip. Address your envelopes, inner and outer, *before* you assemble your invitations and put them in the envelopes. You'll find that addressing empty envelopes is much easier and neater than addressing stuffed ones. Additionally, there won't be any "pressure impression" from the tip of a pen.

ADDRESS SUCCESS

Ready to address your invitations? Follow these guidelines:

Outer envelope: Address formally. Include the complete mailing address. Don't abbreviate city or state and don't use punctuation at the end of lines. Do abbreviate Mr., Mrs., Jr., and Dr.

For a married couple with different last names, or an unmarried couple living together, send one invitation with names listed alphabetically. On the outer envelope, an "and" should be inserted between the names of a married couple but not between the unmarried couple.

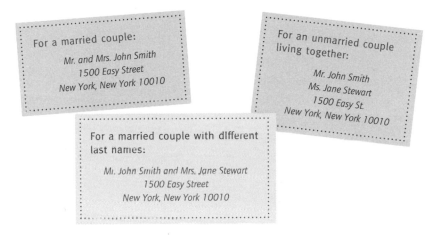

For a married couple:

Mr. and Mrs. John Smith
1500 Easy Street
New York, New York 10010

For an unmarried couple living together:

Mr. John Smith
Ms. Jane Stewart
1500 Easy St.
New York, New York 10010

For a married couple with different last names:

Mr. John Smith and Mrs. Jane Stewart
1500 Easy Street
New York, New York 10010

Inner Envelope: Address formally, but don't use first names or the mailing address. For an unmarried couple that does not live together but will be attending as a couple, send separate invitations to their homes. If you're unable to get both addresses, use format for unmarried couple (below) and send invitation to the address you have.

For a married couple:

Mr. and Mrs. Smith

For a married couple with different last names or an unmarried couple living together:

Mr. Smith and Mrs. (Ms.) Stewart

If children are invited, the parents' names only are written on the outer envelope. Children's first names are written below their parents' names on the inner envelope.

For example: Mr. and Mrs. Smith

Mary and John

The anatomy of a formal invitation is as follows:

- Outer envelope, usually lined
- Ceremony invitation card
- Inner envelope
- Reception card (if the reception location is not the same as the ceremony location)
- Reply card with a preaddressed, stamped envelope

The anatomy of an informal invitation looks like this:

- Outer envelope
- Invitation card with reception information
- Inner envelope (optional)
- Ceremony and reception information sheet with directions
- Reply card with preaddressed, stamped envelope

To assemble your formal invitation:

1. Place enclosures (reception card or other inserts) on top of the invitation, or in the fold of the invitation. A piece of tissue, provided by the printer, may be placed between the invitation and the enclosures.

2. Reply cards go under the flap of the reply envelope and then over the invitation or inside the fold.

3. The invitation, together with the enclosures, is put in the inner envelope (the smaller envelope) with the spine side (if you're using a folded invitation) or left side toward the bottom and with the front of the invitation facing the back of the envelope. The inner envelope is then placed in the outer envelope (unsealed) with the front facing the outer envelope's flap.

To assemble your informal invitation:

1. Place enclosures on top of the invitation, or in the fold of the invitation.

2. Reply cards go under the flap of the reply envelope and then over the invitation or inside the fold.

3. Place the information sheet on top of the reply card, with the church information before the reception details.

4. The invitation, together with the enclosures, is put in the inner envelope (although many informal invitations don't have one).

New Rules of the Road

The Invitation: FORGING YOUR OWN PATH

We don't live in the 1800s, so why should we follow antiquated wedding-invitation rules? Here are some fabulous modern ideas for Anti-Bride-style (and still perfectly proper) wedding invitations.

THE TWIST	TWISTING WITHOUT TRAUMA
Use only one envelope— no lining, no double envelopes.	By using only one envelope, you're not only simplifying the cumbersome process of putting the invitation together but saving a few bucks as well.
Include your ceremony and reception information together on the same invitation card.	If you plan to include your entire clan in both your ceremony and reception, just print up one card—why kill trees when you don't have to?
Make your reply card a postcard.	A stamped, preaddressed postcard makes responding even easier for your guests, and it costs you less (no envelopes to order, and less postage to buy).

Hip Tip. Get creative with paper stock. Use colored or translucent paper, rice paper, road maps, or diffused photos to create your signature invitation. Using pretty, oversized postage stamps is a no-cost, highbrow way to decorate the carrier envelope—check with your post office for the latest designs. Multitask by inquiring whether your invitation will require extra postage—some invitation envelopes are larger than the standard size, so it costs extra to mail them. You definitely don't want your invitations to arrive in your guests' mailboxes with postage due.

GIVE YOUR INVITATION A PERSONAL TOUCH

If the standard engraved invitation isn't for you, use your imagination to create a work of art that suits your wedding style. Having a romantic storybook wedding? Present your guests with a parchment scroll worthy of Cinderella. Planning a tropical island wedding? How about printing your invitation as an illustrated map of your island destination? The ideas below should get you brainstorming:

- Cool black-and-white photo montage of the two of you printed on the invitation cover

- A vintage postcard of your destination color-copied on heavy card stock and glued to the front of a preprinted invitation, tied with a coordinating ribbon

- A historical map of the city where you met or where you'll be honeymooning printed on the cover of the invitation

- A vintage fruit-crate label, with your names pasted in (using Photoshop), printed on the invitation cover

- A family photo, baby pictures of the two of you, or another favorite image, lithographed on card stock (add a vellum overlay and you've created something frameable)

- Strong metallic ink printed on colored card stock

- Handmade paper flecked with floral pieces with letterpress printing

OH, BEHAVE! In your zeal to cut the fat from your invitation, don't omit crucial information that would affect guest comfort. For example, if the invitation doesn't make it clear that the wedding's outdoors, add to the information sheet any necessary advice, such as "Ladies may prefer to wear flat shoes in case of uneven ground at the beachfront ceremony."

Sticky Situations

Wedding invitations involve some decidedly old-fashioned customs, many of which make little sense to us modern gals. Making complex real-life situations conform to these rigid customs can be vexing. Here are some dilemmas you might encounter, and our suggested solutions.

You want to have a small, family-only ceremony and a larger reception that includes friends and extended family.

Solution: To invite people to the reception only, word the invitation as follows: "Mr. and Mrs. Ron Smith request the pleasure of your company at the wedding reception of their daughter . . ." If someone asks for an explanation, just tell them, "We decided to do a ceremony with only our immediate families," or "The chapel we're being married in can only accommodate twenty people so we decided on a family-only ceremony." No one should be offended—many ceremonies occur in small places where only a handful can attend.

You want to invite adults only, no children.

Solution: This *is* a touchy subject. Even when you address your invitation to the parents only, with no mention of the children, some guests won't get the hint and will assume that their children are welcome. The best way to prevent confusion and misunderstandings is to address the envelope to the parents only, and on the preprinted reply card make it clear that you expect grown ups only.

For example: *M_____ _____ and my adult guest*

M_____ _____ will ____ attend

If parents call to complain, simply tell them that for budgetary reasons you can't accommodate the children of friends and family. If you like, you can offer to arrange for a nanny service, to be paid for either by you or by the guests with children.

You and your partner have a child and you want to include his name on the invitation.

Solution: If you want to include the child as part of the invitation, here's one example of how to word it:

> *Ruby Smith*
> *and*
> *Christopher Reese*
>
> *along with their son,*
> *Jack,*
>
> *invite you to attend*
> *their marriage . . .*

Note that if your child is attending the wedding and you've made it clear that guests' children are not welcome, some guests may balk, especially if they've gone to great lengths to find and hire a babysitter for the occasion. We say, it's your party and it's your family. Do what you want.

You want to address an invitation to someone in the process of a divorce and name change.

Solution: She can be addressed by her married name (Mrs. Jane Smith) or her maiden name (Ms. Jane Lewis). The best solution is to ask her how she prefers to be addressed.

Your wedding is canceled after the invitations are sent.

Solution: If the wedding is called off a month or more before the date, send a card with the following wording:

> *Mr. and Mrs. John Smith*
> *announce that the marriage of their daughter*
>
> *Ruby Ann Smith*
> *to*
> *Christopher John Reese*
>
> *will not take place*

If the wedding is canceled less than a month before the scheduled date and time is short, a telephone call is fine.

You've just had your invitations printed and your in-laws are upset because their names aren't on them.

Solution: If they're concerned about etiquette, let them know that listing only the bride's parents on the wedding invitation, especially for a more formal wedding, is the traditional route. Gently explain that they are just as much a part of the wedding as your parents are and that you were following traditional etiquette when you worded the invitation the way you did. However, if it's a money issue—they paid for half, for example—then they may have a legitimate gripe. In this case, reprinting, on your dime, is probably your best option. The best strategy, of course, is to prevent the problem in the first place: Before you order the invitations, ask them if they expect their names to appear on the invitation, especially if they are heavy campaign contributors.

One or both of your parents are deceased, and you don't know how to word your formal invitation.

Solution: Here's how it should read.

If one parent (in this case the mother) is deceased:	If both parents are deceased, then word it this way.
Mr. Ron Smith requests the honor of your presence at the marriage of his daughter Ruby Ann to Christopher John Reese . . .	Ruby Ann Smith daughter of the late Mr. and Mrs. Ron Smith and Mr. and Mrs. Robert Reese request the honor of your presence at the marriage of Ruby Ann and Christopher John . . .

CHAPTER 5

THE WEDDING PARTY

The wedding party is traditionally a coterie of the best people in your life—sisters, cousins, neighbors, and friends—the people you've really bonded with. But when it comes to choosing your bridal attendants, these relationships can suddenly seem complicated—for example, if your best friend is more of a sister to you than your real sister is. Your college roommate may be raising a soccer team in Wichita, and you may now have an urban family composed of roommates, co-workers, and friends that reflects your current lifestyle and emotional needs. Negotiating the differences between your present and past lifestyles can be a challenge, particularly if you've changed locations, socio-economic brackets, or education levels.

The Anti-Bride strategy is simple: Get down the aisle in style without burning any bridges, and do it on *your* terms. This chapter takes you though the sometimes prickly task of choosing the people in your wedding party, identifying each person's responsibilities, and treating your crew with the respect and love they deserve. You'll learn all about the traditions that come with choosing bridal attendants and the duties customarily assigned to them, and you'll get the scoop on how to properly soothe ruffled feathers when you don't (or do) go the traditional route.

However you go about choosing attendants, understand that the job of a bridesmaid is serious business. The people in your bridal party need to have thick skin and nerves of steel, and they must be up to the challenge, mentally and financially. Choose them wisely and early in the game. They'll be able to use the lead time to find ways to save money on things like travel and apparel—and you'll be able to use the lead time to develop a Plan B if they need to exit for some reason.

The Golden Rules

The traditional bridal party includes parents, attendants, and supporting cast (flower girl and ring bearer). In times past, the number of bridesmaids included in a wedding depended on how big and formal the wedding was: the bigger the wedding, the larger the group of attendants. In a conventional wedding, the maid of honor slot is usually given to a sister (the bride's or the groom's), while bridesmaid slots are reserved for other siblings, close relatives, and maybe a friend or two. If she's sticking to old-fashioned wedding etiquette, the bride doesn't have much say in the attendant selection process.

The number of attendants in a wedding party isn't set in stone—an average wedding (150 guests or more) typically has four to six bridal attendants and around three ushers or groomsmen. The number of ushers is usually one for every 50 guests.

Time Capsule. In ancient Rome, bridesmaids dressed in attire similar to the bride's, hoping to confuse evil spirits trying to kidnap her.

The Chosen People . . . THE TRADITION

Before you decide on who you want to stand up for you, you might want to know what functions these people actually perform. To outline who does what, here are the duties usually assigned to each member of the wedding party.

Hip Tip. Like the maid of honor, the best man (or woman) has an important role as the groom's right-hand man, taking care of myriad tasks before and during the wedding festivities. Because the typical groom doesn't usually make it a priority to study wed-iquette, the best man often doesn't know what the groom expects of him. To ensure your mental health (and your relationship with your sweetie), come up with a Cliffs Notes version of Best Man duties. The list can be a starting point for both guys to use when they hash out the details over a beer. Let them take it from there, and trust them to do their best.

WEDDING PARTY MEMBERS' OFFICIAL DUTIES

WHO	RESPONSIBILITIES
Bride's Parents	MOTHER • Spreads the word about the registry • Helps bride shop for gown • Stands in the receiving line FATHER • Escorts bride down the aisle • Stands in the receiving line • Dances with his daughter after her first dance with the groom BOTH • Assist in creating the guest list • Toast the couple at the rehearsal dinner
Groom's Parents	• Host the rehearsal dinner • May pay for the liquor and bar service at the reception • Stand in the receiving line
Bride's Honor Attendant (i.e., Maid or Matron of Honor)	• Helps with bride's and bridesmaids' dress fittings • Calls vendors and sets up appointments for bride as requested, keeps bridesmaids up to speed, addresses invitations, and cohosts shower with bridesmaids • Attends rehearsal and rehearsal dinner • Keeps the bride looking her best: helps her dress on the wedding day, arranges her veil and train before and during the ceremony, and helps her change into her "getaway" outfit • During the ceremony, walks in the processional, and stands next to the bride at the altar and in the receiving line • Holds bridal bouquet and groom's ring during the ceremony • Signs the marriage certificate as a witness • Bustles the bride's gown and helps arrange or remove the veil before the reception • Sits to the right of the bride during reception, dances with the best man, and assists the bride whenever necessary • After the wedding, helps the best man bring the gifts to the bride and groom's home and brings the wedding gown to a dry cleaner's shop specified by the bride

WEDDING PARTY MEMBERS' OFFICIAL DUTIES, continued

WHO	RESPONSIBILITIES
Bridesmaid	• Acts as second in command—takes direction from maid or matron of honor • Helps plan the bridal shower • Attends rehearsal and rehearsal dinner • During the ceremony, walks behind the ushers in the processional, stands next to the maid or matron of honor at the altar, walks down the aisle with an usher in the recessional, and stands next to the maid or matron of honor in the receiving line • Helps guide the flower girl or ring bearer, if needed • Sits at the head table with the bride and groom at the reception
Groom's Honor Attendant (i.e., Best Man)	• Has the foresight and good sense not to host the bachelor party the night before the ceremony or rehearsal dinner • Helps groom choose wedding clothes and makes sure his other attendants get fitted • Sets up appointments for groom and ushers as requested, organizes transportation to and from the ceremony and reception for the couple and bridal party, hosts and organizes bachelor party, and confirms honeymoon travel arrangements • Keeps the groom looking good—helps him dress before the ceremony • During the ceremony, stands next to the groom at the altar and escorts maid or matron of honor down the aisle in the recessional • Holds the bride's ring, marriage license, and officiant's fee during the ceremony • Sits at the head table with the bride and groom at the reception and makes the first toast • Distributes tips to vendors on behalf of the reception hosts • Deals with the drunk and disorderly at the reception • With the maid of honor, delivers the gifts to the bride and groom's home after the reception, and returns groom's and ushers' rented clothing

WHO	RESPONSIBILITIES
Usher or Groomsman	• Rolls out the aisle runner in church (if applicable) • Seats guests before the ceremony • Escorts the mothers of the bride and groom to their seats • Stands next to the best man in the ceremony, and escorts a bridesmaid down the aisle in the recessional
Flower Girl	• Walks down the aisle before the bride in the processional and recessional, scattering flower petals from a basket (or carrying a pomander)
Ring Bearer	• Walks down the aisle just before the flower girl in the processional and recessional, carrying a small decorative pillow with two rings tied to it (usually fakes)

New Rules of the Road

As the CEO of the most monumental project of her life, the Anti-Bride isn't afraid to buck tradition—especially when it comes to picking the members of her supreme team. The time-honored rule that sisters, sisters-in-law, and even cousins are automatic shoo-ins is history! Including a cousin you rarely talk to, or a sister you have issues with, just to keep the peace is not what your day is all about. We can almost hear the screams from Emily Post's grave as we make the following suggestion, but you could even forgo the concept of the maid of honor altogether. Instead you could create a peaceful wedding-party atmosphere by having each attendant perform a specific, honored task (and nix the matching outfits). Those who stand with you as you say your vows should be the people who love, cherish, and support you—the people who make you feel good—not necessarily your sister or cousin. So if the person you feel closest to (besides your fiancé) is your male downstairs neighbor or a co-worker at your tattoo salon, feel free to include him or her in your wedding party. There's no need to be emotionally blackmailed by outdated rules.

The Chosen People . . . FORGING YOUR OWN PATH

When you're selecting your bridal party, clarity, self-knowledge, and brutal honesty are what will help you identify the right women (or men) for the job. Imagine that you're picking people to help you launch a new business. Whom in your life would you want to work with? Our list would include people whom we can count on, people who value our time as much as their own, people who can bring specific skills and abilities (as well as talent, love, support, and flexibility) to the table, and people who are pinch hitters and good in a crisis.

Your best guys and girls should meet the following criteria:

- **Be near and dear to you.** They've seen you at your worst and know how you handle stress, but they love you anyway.

- **Know you might forget to say thanks (egads!).** Despite your good intentions, you might overlook some of your friends' hard work. The best bridal attendants will overlook your "bridezilla" moments and take the higher ground in a conflict. Think of this as social insurance.

- **Be large and in charge.** Your crew members know you're the director of the show (and that their negative opinions should not be spoken), but they'll know when to offer an ingenious idea you can use.

- **Be expert project managers.** Obnoxious mother-in-law-to-be? Your best girls or guys should know when and how to run interference. Lots of plates in the air? Your team's organization skills are key, and the best and brightest will know to jump in and help when you're having *a day*.

WHEN FRIENDS (AND RELATIVES) ATTACK . . .

If you follow the guidelines listed above, you'll be supported by a group of smart, loving, responsible, fun individuals. Or you might even choose not to have any attendants—it's your prerogative. The downside of flouting tradition here, though, is the potential for ruffling feathers. The possibility of offending someone who incorrectly assumed they would be an anointed member of the wedding is huge. As you may have already discovered, people become complex, passive-aggressive, and just plain weird when it comes to weddings.

When your usually supportive friends and family members start acting strange before your wedding, consider what might be going on with them. Your best friends, while happy for you, may be worried that they're losing you forever.

Your ex, who's now a friend, may not be able to imagine life without you (and finds himself especially upset at the thought of you in another man's arms). Your favorite gay friend from the office may fear he will be subjected to brunch with the hetero couples for eternity and that he's lost his gal pal. Your mom may not approve of your motorcycle-mechanic honey, or your dad may be taking issue with your decision to walk down the aisle with a woman.

Whatever the case may be, repeat after us: "I accept other people's lifestyles and choices, and I deserve the same respect—especially on my wedding day! Detractors, naysayers, and emotionally toxic people must behave or be removed from the proceedings. Period."

When dealing with someone who is feeling a little freaked out about your wedding (whether or not they admit it), take this person aside and gently stress how you feel, but also emphasize how important he or she is to you. And, while things may be a little awkward between you, it's important to invest some time, love, and energy in order to maintain the bonds that you've built. By acting as a beacon in the wilderness of passive-aggressive human tendencies, you will lead by example and hopefully dispel any negative energy. Here are some possible "scripts" to guide you when you are utterly stumped by friends' and relatives' perplexing behavior.

Friendship Vow of Honor (to best friend, singleton, partner in crime)

I, _____, do solemnly swear to attend ladies' night or trashy-magazine-pedicure-gossip day a minimum of once per month. I won't bore you with how deliriously happy I am and I will always be there to hear about cads you may be dating or office romances that are going nowhere. In the event that I get pregnant, I won't subject you to play-by-play reports of hormonal changes in my body.

Friendship Vow of Honor (to best gay male office buddy)

I, _____, do solemnly swear to attend trashy TV night one night per month, and/or a gossipy Bloody Mary–infused brunch. I will not bore you with how deliriously happy I am and will always be there to hear about your romantic flings and book-proposal or screenplay rejection slips. I will not subject you to hetero happy-couple brunches or turn into a Stepford Wife.

Familial Vow of Honor (to Mom and Dad)

I, _____, do solemnly swear to always keep the lines of communication open, no matter what your feelings are toward my partner. While this person may not be the sort of mate you had in mind for me, I will try to demonstrate over time why he/she makes my life complete. I promise to love and support you and your lifestyle choices.

The Ten Commandments
(OF NOT TORTURING YOUR BRIDESMAIDS)

So you've selected your team: a group of loyal, good-hearted, fun-loving, and organized people. You love them dearly, and you're counting on them to support you during this exciting and stressful time. To keep your bridesmaids happy, love, honor, and obey these commandments:

1. **Ask; don't assume.** Being a bridesmaid involves a mountain of responsibilities, relationship issues, time commitments, and financial burdens. *Ask* potential candidates if they can be a part of your wedding, and provide them with a cost estimate.

2. **Remember who's wearing the bridesmaid dress.** If you choose a bias-cut sheath that's meant for a size-4 body, the size-12 new mom in your crew may clock you with her breast pump.

3. **Know that money is always an object.** If the dress you love is $400 and your bridesmaids have just started paying back their student loans, kick a little subsidy their way—in the end, even your cash-strapped pals will love a swanky dress they can wear again. If you can't contribute, change the dress.

4. **Xena, you're not the center of the universe.** They're happy for you, but they have lives too, and they won't want to discuss caterers and flower arranging every time they see you.

5. **Don't channel Martha.** If you ask bridesmaids to pick a dress in the "wisteria" color family, you'll only multiply their stress as they try to hunt it down. Be specific about what you want. Or go to a paint store and get color swatches to help guide your gals.

6. **It's your party (but you can't cry if you want to).** If your bridesmaids throw you a shower or a bachelorette party, let them plan it. It's okay to give a gentle nudge in the right direction, but make no demands.

7. **Remember that greed isn't good.** If people are throwing you multiple showers or other parties, your bridesmaids (and others who are invited to more than one shower) don't need to buy more than one gift or even attend all events.

8. **Control your inner control freak.** Have faith that your best pals will surely handle their wedding responsibilities with grace and enthusiasm. Just give them a list of duties, trust, and back off.

9. **Know thyself.** Bridal indecisiveness is the biggest pet peeve of most bridesmaids we've asked. Having a game plan will reduce everyone's stress.

10. **Cultivate good karma.** When it's their turn, they *will* remember if it was a pleasure or a pain in the butt to be a part of your big day!

DON'T LET THIS HAPPEN TO YOU!

Jill has a lesson for us all: When planning your big day, go with your gut about whom you want and make sure everyone understands how you want things done, no matter what seems proper. In high school, Jill and her two best friends each pledged to stand up for the others on their wedding days. True to her word, when her two friends married soon after graduation, Jill happily donned the taffeta. Fifteen years later, when Jill was making plans for her own nuptials, she remembered the promise she'd made. Despite having become distant from her two high-school pals, she got back in touch with them and asked them to be her bridesmaids, along with her two current best friends and her sister.

The problems began with the dress. Some members of the group liked it, others didn't, and most thought $150 was way too much to spend. Then came the pre-wedding parties. Her sister, the maid of honor, who knew nothing about wedding etiquette, didn't really understand what kind of shower and bachelorette party Jill wanted and wound up giving the wrong information to the collective. Partly because Jill wasn't entirely clear about her wishes, and partly because her two high-school friends didn't know her very well anymore, a game of "telephone" ensued and she ended up with a cookie-cutter shower and drunken last hurrah. Frustrated and angry, she vented on some wedding message boards on the Internet, using a fictitious name. Unfortunately, some of her bridesmaids ran across the postings and recognized them as hers. By the time of the wedding, nobody in her wedding party was speaking to her. Her advice for brides? "Choose your attendants judiciously, be clear about your expectations, realize that perfection is unattainable, and try to have a sense of humor." Our advice? Be clear with your attendants about your wishes and employ net-iquette on Internet message boards!

Hip Tip. Enlist someone to be your "shadow" on your big day—your trusted secret-agent girl. Need someone to run to the store to get you a new pair of nude hose, keep track of your bouquet (you're *going* to set it down somewhere and forget where you put it), snag you a plate of delectable canapés before they're consumed, and get you a glass of champagne when you're parched? She's got you covered.

HONORING THE ATTENDANTS (AND KEEPING THEIR EXPENSES IN CHECK)

To get an idea of how much money your attendants will be shelling out, review the cost estimates below. We've also included some money-saving ideas to help reduce their expenses.

Expenditure	Estimate	Cost-Cutting Tip
DRESS	$100 to $500	Rent dresses; check out Bluefly.com or eBay; shop off the rack at discount stores (e.g., Marshalls) or department store outlets (e.g., Nordstrom Rack, Saks Off 5th); negotiate bulk discounts at a bridal salon; or let the girls shop for their own dress in the color family of your choice.
LINGERIE	$50 to $75	Shop discount stores (e.g., Target and K-Mart) for strapless bras, panty hose, and slips. Check Macy's lingerie sales.
SHOES	$30 to $50	You could check out stores like Payless for dyeable shoes (although chances are, your friends already have a pair in their closet gathering dust that they can have dyed again). Or, nix the matching shoes altogether and go with neutral metallic or black strappy styles (the universal bridesmaid-shoe problem solver, says Bridget Brown of Bella Bridesmaids in San Francisco).
JEWELRY AND ACCESSORIES	$50 to $100	Have a local bead-shop owner or jeweler create a look for each bridesmaid, and give them the jewelry as a gift.

Hip Tip. If your best friend is a man and he wants to stand with you on your wedding day, ask him to be a bridal attendant! Just don't require him to act or dress like a woman (unless your nuptials are a trannyfest), and don't call him a "bridesmaid"— "honor attendant" or simply "attendant" will do. Use good judgment and sensitivity when giving him responsibilities. Bustling your dress might be overkill.

Expenditure	Estimate	Cost-Cutting Tip
HAIR AND MAKEUP	$50 to $150	If you want everyone's coiffure to match, book an appointment with a stylist and pick up the tab. If it's not in your budget and you need your bridesmaids to cover their hair-care costs, hire a stylist at an agreed-upon cost or trust them to take care of their look themselves.
TRAVEL TO WEDDING CITY	$500 to $1000	If your attendants will be paying for their own travel and lodging expenses, give them plenty of time to make travel plans and save up their frequent-flier miles. Arrange for bulk discounts at hotels, have bridesmaids double up to cut costs, or set them up at friends' houses to avoid hotel fees entirely. Arrange transportation to and from the airport (with attractive single male friends pressed into service) so that they can avoid pricey car rentals or shuttle buses.
BACHELORETTE PARTY AND/OR SHOWER	$50 to $200 per bridesmaid	Tell the maid of honor that you want to consider the bridesmaids' pocketbooks, and that a low-key celebration would be just fine with you. Suggest that your bridesmaids consolidate the two events— a shower–bachelorette party combo. (To really save them money, don't bar-hop—those $7 drinks are budget killers,.) Propose a small, intimate dinner, or a cocktail party, complete with nibbles and a signature drink or an inexpensive wine tasting, at someone's home. Activities such as a massage therapy session and a great B-movie screening accompanied by theme food may be just the ticket!
SHOWER AND WEDDING GIFTS	$50 to $200	Let your bridesmaids know that their presence and support are the best gifts you could ever receive.

Attendant Alternatives

Being the socially conscious Anti-Bride that you are, you want to make *everyone* (not just your bridesmaids) feel included in your community, right? Well, if you can find ways to de-emphasize the exclusive, *in-crowd* nature of the wedding party (which is emphasized by those match-ey dresses), you're halfway there. Instead of focusing undue attention on who's a bridesmaid and who isn't, emphasize "honor duties" and important tasks that can be performed by friends and family. Below are some tasks you can assign to these key people to help them feel included in the festivities (bestow thanks accordingly!):

- Act as the bride's "shadow" for the day, making sure all needs are met.
- Stay on top of the weather and bring a few extra umbrellas if it looks like rain.
- Give rides to and from the wedding to out-of-towners and other guests.
- Spice up the reception space or make wedding favors.
- Sing, do a reading, or make a toast at the ceremony or reception.
- Arrive early at the reception space and make sure things like tables, chairs, decorations, and champagne are in place.
- Pick up flowers from the ceremony and take them to the reception.
- Make sure the bride's and groom's personal things (coats, purse, wedding-day emergency kit) are safe and sound.
- Be a "meet-and-greeter" at the reception.
- Serve refreshments or wedding cake.
- Pass out rice or birdseed.
- Keep track of wedding gifts, making sure a gift card is taped or tied to each gift, and help the best man transport them to the couple's home after the reception.

AND THE ULTIMATE ATTENDANT ALTERNATIVE... NO ATTENDANTS!

Yes, you do have this option. You can fly solo, without any attendants at all. Some ways around the "official duties" that come with the bridesmaid's job include relying on a wedding consultant, who could make sure you make every appointment and be your girl Friday on the big day. But that's going to cost you. Even with extra help from family and a hired right-hand person, you might find that some details still fall through the cracks. And, as hokey as the bridal-attendant tradition may seem, weddings seem to call for people to get involved in pre-scripted ways. Although you might not miss being surrounded by a bunch of squealing women in evening gowns, they might feel a little left out (yet many actually heave a sigh of relief).

Sticky Situations

You're thrilled to be getting married, and you're hoping that your friends and relatives will be equally enthusiastic. But what if they're not? What if they object to your choices? How do you handle these conflicts without offending them? Here are some mannerly solutions to common wedding party problems.

Your family doesn't want to be involved.

Solution: Whether it's a lifestyle, cultural, or financial issue that's causing your relatives to feel this way, it's important that you communicate how you feel about their being a part of your day. If they don't respond in a positive way, you may have to count them out emotionally or financially. This is where your friends come in, taking on more integral roles in the planning and ceremony. Yes, it will hurt, and you'll feel like something's missing, but you need to be surrounded by those who truly support your union.

One or more of your bridesmaids is fiscally challenged and is having trouble with the mounting expenses for her dress, shoes, flight, and hotel room.

Solution: This is a common situation. Frustration about financial circumstances often creates tension for everyone involved. If you can afford to help her out, do so. This is your day, but it's also her life—she is incurring expenses for your benefit. If you can't contribute, help her come up with low-cost options. Choose less expensive attire (or let all the bridesmaids wear what they want!) and help her find a discount flight and place to stay. In the process, you'll convey the important place she holds in your life, while letting her know that it's not all about the money.

You're being pressured to ask a relative to be in your wedding party.

Solution: If you were to stick to tradition, you'd never pick a friend over a relative, such as your partner's sister, but we say, you should go with your gut and pick whoever means the most to you. Our suggestion? Let the relative in question know that you love her but you feel a need to include your best friends, who are your day-to-day tribe. Characterize your decision as a break to her—tell her you can't imagine that she'd really enjoy planning parties and going to dress fittings with a bunch of people she doesn't know. Discuss other possible roles she could play instead. Chances are that she may be relieved not to have to plunk down the big bucks for that bridesmaid dress.

A bridesmaid isn't working out and you need to replace her.

Solution: Honesty is the best policy. First, mention that she seems unhappy in her role and see if she offers an explanation. She might be feeling pressured by all of her bridesmaid responsibilities, or might be having relationship, work, or financial issues that have nothing to do with you. Offer to release her from her obligation and suggest another role. If she won't abdicate, go in for the close. Communicate that you love her as a friend, but she's not posting and it's causing stress, so you need to ask her to bow out. Make it clear that this turn of events won't affect your friendship with her (although it probably will).

A bridesmaid has abdicated, and you want to ask a friend to take over without having her feel like "sloppy seconds."

Solution: Be honest: Tell her that you wanted her initially, but you felt pressured to choose your college roommate. You now have a vacancy and want to follow your heart. Say that if she would consider it, you'd be honored. Be warned that she might have felt relief rather than regret when passed over, so don't be surprised if she doesn't jump at the offer. Respect her answer.

A friend assumes she'll be your maid of honor, although you don't intend to ask her.

Solution: Almost anything you might say will probably hurt her, but you need to exalt the friendship and not throw the baby out with the bathwater. Be honest and sensitive to your friend's point of view, but stand firm. For example, you might say, "I know we've been friends since we were kids, but when I moved to Chicago, I felt very isolated and Karen really helped me with the transition. I consider her to be a constant in my current life, which is why I want her standing up with me. I hope you understand." An even better approach might be a practical one (with a hint of flattery thrown in for good measure): "Since you've got so many important responsibilities already, with your family and your demanding career, I can't imagine that you would have time to do all of the things that go along with being a bridesmaid. Karen's job is only part-time, and she has a lot of free time on her hands, so she seemed like a logical choice."

You're not sure what duties you should assign to your male attendant.

Solution: While a male attendant can do a variety of tasks, he will probably prefer to steer clear of girl-type jobs like helping you into your dress or bustling your gown at the reception. Most likely, he'll also want to avoid the all female bridal showers (so why not make the shower coed?). He could, however, walk down the aisle with the bridesmaids and stand with them during the ceremony. If female bridesmaids are being escorted down the aisle in the recessional, the male attendant can go unaccompanied or he can walk with a non-bridesmaid female (e.g., a grandmother, aunt, or cousin).

CHAPTER 6

ATTIRE

The right outfit is equal parts glamour and guts. The word to keep in mind when picking your ensemble is *appropriateness,* the cornerstone of looking socially acceptable and *correct* for your immediate situation and surroundings. Somewhere in between Lady Di's "crumpled-tissue" wedding gown and the Burning Man dreadlocks, corset, and motorcycle boots look is a style that's stunning, appropriate, and uniquely your own.

The question for many women isn't What's my style? but What's my bridal style? As you try on dress after dress, you may ask yourself, Do I look like a cookie-cutter bride, or have I gone too far (or not far enough)? Will my look be appropriate in my surroundings and venue? Does my style correspond with that of my groom? How do I coordinate the look if he's not supposed to see my dress? Addressing these vexing questions is the focus of this chapter, which will help you tackle the job of picking that perfect wedding ensemble and making sure it works with your body type and coloring, the location of your soiree, and the type of weather you expect.

The Golden Rules

Wedding Wear: THE TRADITION

Who	Informal (Day)	Semiformal (Day)	Formal (Day)
Bride	Simple dress (white or pastel, street length or shorter) or tailored suit; short veil or headpiece; no train; simple bouquet	Dress of any length (white or pastel); short veil; no train; small bouquet	Floor-length or shorter gown with a chapel, sweep, or detachable train and matching shoes; headpiece or veil; full bouquet
Groom	Suit; dress shirt (white, colored, or striped); four-in-hand (straight) tie	Suit (to complement the bride's attire); dress shirt (white, colored, or striped); four-in-hand (straight) tie	Gray stroller, waistcoat, and striped pants; dress shirt; striped tie; gloves optional
Bridesmaid	Seasonal suit or dress (matching optional); small bouquet	Street-length dress or shorter (matching optional); small bouquet	Floor or street-length dress with matching shoes; short veil or headpiece; gloves optional (bride decides); similar accessories; bouquet
Groomsman or Usher	Suit; dress shirt (white, colored, or striped); four-in-hand (straight) tie	Suit (to complement the groom's attire); dress shirt (white, colored, or striped); four-in-hand (straight) tie	Gray stroller, waistcoat, and striped pants (to complement the groom's attire); dress shirt; striped tie; gloves optional
Mothers of Bride and Groom	Dress or suit that complements the other mother's attire	Dress or suit that complements the other mother's attire	Elegant dress or suit, usually street length, that complements the other mother's attire; hair ornament or hat; gloves optional
Fathers of Bride and Groom	Suit that matches the groomsmen's or ushers' attire	Suit or tuxedo that matches the groomsmen's or ushers' attire	Black or white tuxedo that matches the groomsmen/ushers' attire

Whether you consider yourself to be a traditional bride, a fearless rebel, or something in between, your wedding will fall into one of three categories: informal, semiformal, and formal. The rule of thumb is this: the less formal you go, the more fashion forward your choices may be (but this isn't to say that a super-formal wedding can't be quirky). Use the following as a guide, and break the rules as you see fit.

Informal (Evening)	Semiformal (Evening)	Formal (Evening)
Simple dress (white or pastel, street length or shorter) or tailored suit, short veil or headpiece; no train; simple bouquet; Sassy cocktail dress okay	Dress of any length (white or pastel) with matching shoes; veil elbow-length or shorter; bouquet simpler than that used in formal wedding	Floor-length gown, long sleeved, sleeveless, or strapless, with a chapel, sweep, or detachable train; gloves optional; veil of any length; full bouquet
Dark suit; dress shirt (white, colored, or striped); four-in-hand (straight) tie	Suit (to complement the bride's attire); dress shirt (white, colored, or striped); four-in-hand (straight) tie	Tuxedo, or dark dinner jacket with matching trousers; dress shirt; bow tie; vest or cummerbund; white or ivory jacket over dark trousers for summery climates
Cocktail dress or suit (matching optional); small bouquet	Street-length dress or shorter (matching optional); small bouquet	Floor-length dress with matching shoes; short veil or headpiece; gloves optional (bride decides); similar accessories, bouquet
Suit; dress shirt (white, colored, or striped); four-in-hand (straight) tie	Suit (to complement the groom's attire); dress shirt (white, colored, or striped); four-in-hand (straight) tie	Tuxedo, or dark dinner jacket with matching trousers; dress shirt, bow tie; vest or cummerbund; white or ivory jacket over dark trousers for summery climates
Dress or suit that complements the other mother's attire	Street-length dress that complements the other mother's attire	Long evening or dinner dress that complements other mother's attire; shoes, hair ornament or hat; gloves optional
Suit that matches the groomsmen's or ushers' attire	Suit or tuxedo that matches the groomsmen's or ushers' attire	Black or white tuxedo that matches the groomsmen/ushers' attire

New Rules of the Road

There's a certain amount of fashion leadership that the truly chic possess—the ability to bend rather than break the rules. Consider Sharon Stone in a black Gap turtleneck and ball skirt amidst the sequins at the Oscars, and Brigitte Bardot in her trademark white trench and updo (and little else). These women have defined fashion improvisation, breaking the rules and getting away with it.

But what about the rest of us? We've all been to an informal cocktail party where that one poor soul (who either didn't check with the hostess, or doesn't get out much) is skulking in the corner in a dress with a plunging neckline and over-the-top jewelry. Or we've attended a shorts-and-T-shirt backyard barbecue where that one woman is dressed like Daisy Buchanan in her large straw hat and frothy silk floral. We can't condemn these women for giving it their best effort. But society being the arbiter of "good taste" that it is, the rules governing what's right or "not quite" are always shifting. Too much pressure for you? Not at all! Anti-Brides welcome the challenge to be chic, sleek, *and* unique on their wedding day.

The trick is to incorporate your personal style in your wedding garb while keeping your eye on what's appropriate. Tradition tells us that evening weddings are usually formal, so you might opt for a longer train, cocktail swank, or baring more skin. But morning or early afternoon ceremonies are usually considered less formal, so you might want to lose the beading, train, and décolletage.

Location is another factor. A bare, backless silk sheath may be perfect for a beach wedding but might be a little too slinky and "plain Jane" for a formal church wedding. Or, if you're throwing a backyard soiree, you'll probably want to ditch the ten-foot train and gloves unless Dad owns a compound in the Hamptons. Balancing your sense of style, appropriateness, common sense, and surroundings (with a dash of courage) is the key to creating a successful and savvy wedding style.

Wedding Wear: FORGING YOUR OWN PATH

THE TEN COMMANDMENTS OF BRIDAL ATTIRE

1. **Know thyself and the dress will follow.** Know your shape, your height, and your coloring, and have some idea of silhouettes that suit you. The wrong silhouette can accentuate figure flaws, such as an ample derrière or heavy midsection, causing you to feel awkward or unstylish.

2. **Not every runway trend is a "real way" trend.** One concept that is as elusive as the perfect crème brûlée is *chic*, the most misunderstood word in fashion. We say to be chic is about choosing your clothes with thoughtfulness and discretion, and then not thinking another moment about them.

3. **You should be wearing the garment—it should not be wearing you.** Pinching shoes, a tight bodice, a scratchy crinoline, or a constricting corset will make you cranky (and cranky brides don't always exhibit exemplary manners!). Choose garments that transform you in gorgeous ways, not garments that require things that your body can't deliver

4. **Aim for private comforts:** silk undies, a cotton-lined bodice, shoes you can dance in, a dress that doesn't feel like a heavy suit of armor. You will feel more relaxed, you will behave graciously, and you will glow like a candle.

5. **Cleavage is one thing, but *Baywatch* is another.** You want to glide, not bounce down the aisle. Also, think about dancing. Do you want to be one-eighth of an inch away from nipple exposure? Make sure your gown can hold up to the task! Be flashy, but not trashy.

6. **Go light on the makeup.** Tammy Faye couldn't pull off the look, so you shouldn't even try. Makeup artists may pile it on for the photos and longevity, but you'll run the risk of looking embalmed. Know how much makeup you're comfortable wearing, and stand your ground with your makeup artist!

7. **Too many looks (or too much of one look) spoil the look.** Take one or two inspiration points such as shoes, necklace, or beaded bodice and build your look around them. If you have multiple decades going on in a vintage look, or if you appear to be channeling a head-to-toe 1940s war bride, for example, it won't play well, especially in photos. Vintage inspiration is cool, but immersing yourself in a decade that is not your own is a little tragic.

8. **Match your dress to your surroundings.** Look to the setting of your wedding and dress from there: outside or inside, cocktail-lounge funky or Waldorf-Astoria formal—then work with what you've got. A vintage cocktail-lounge look at a woodland wedding might seem like you got off at the wrong stop en route to Palm Springs, circa 1966. Equally inappropriate would be a floor-length $20,000 Vera Wang at your nuptials in your parents' backyard (unless you happen to be a Getty).

9. **White's all right:** Even if it's an encore marriage or you're over forty, white is fine, says Crys Stewart of *Wedding Bells*. (And she says yes to cleavage, too.) Make sure you're comfortable moving and dancing in the dress you've chosen. The only stipulation: if you're over forty, you'll probably want to avoid wearing a virginal veil, traditionally reserved for younger brides.

10. **Despite all the dos and don'ts, have some guts.** You've heard the admonitions: "Your jewelry shouldn't compete with the dress!" "Get completely dressed and then take off one piece of jewelry!" We say, wear a monster tiara if you dare. Just make sure your dress isn't competing with your accessories or you'll end up looking confusing and confused.

BRIDAL JEWELRY

When it comes to choosing jewelry, how much is too much? To enhance your stunning, stylish W-day look without gilding the lily, pick from the following combinations:

- **Shoulder-grazing chandelier earrings with a big, cool bracelet,** *or* **a big, honking necklace with stud earrings.**
- **A tiara and drop earrings and a small bracelet,** *or* **a tiara and a bigger bracelet.**

Keep in mind that if your gown is heavily beaded there's no need to pile on the gear (save for an elegant choker); otherwise you'll look like Queen Elizabeth.

JUSTIFYING THE RED DRESS

Not born of cash but possessing plenty of moxie, Beth is a practicing Wiccan and music journalist. Her first wedding, a large, traditional affair, was done for her family. For her second wedding, Beth wanted to express her style, and what she wanted was *red:* dress, cake, decorations. "Red is the color of luck in Chinese culture. It's my color, and I wanted it everywhere," she says. Enduring comments from relatives ("Oh, she's the different one") and bridesmaids ("So what do we wear this time?"), she smiled sweetly and powered through. She incorporated the colors of the earth signs: fire (red), earth (green), sun (gold), and silver (moon) in her dress and her attendants' dresses. When the day finally arrived, despite the controversy over her color choices, everyone (especially the groom) was astonished at her beauty and Beth was truly and undeniably herself.

DRESS-IQUETTE

Anyone who's been through the bridal gown–shopping experience knows that it can go one of two ways: dumb luck, or worse than a root canal. Here are some surefire ways to swing the odds in your favor and ensure successful apparel-related dealings with your fiancé and with the ateliers you frequent:

- **Set a budget for your ensemble that will not be exceeded.** This will lay the groundwork for solid financial dealings with your future husband.

- **Look in less obvious places.** (Nordstrom Rack, eveningwear) Have an idea of what you want, but be open to new possibilities; look at a range of dress styles, and visualize post-wedding uses (New Year's Eve). Your man will admire your sense of frugality and investment dressing.

- **Remember, time is money.** Utilize the grapevine to avoid dragging your mother and maid of honor into the competitive and estrogen-steeped world of the bridal salon rumble every Saturday for two months. Think of their time as you do your own: precious.

- **Go solo.** You've been picking out your daily attire since kindergarten. So why can't you try on wedding dresses without an entourage? Plan a series of quick, covert trips to bridal salons or dress boutiques on weeknights after work or school (call it "Operation Aisle Style"). The crowds will be thinner, you'll be in a better mood, the salespeople will be in a better mood, and you'll get better service.

- **And the winner is!** Take photos of your final selections (no more than three). Show them to your most stylin' friend and your mom. Schedule an après-work session to try 'em all on. Prepare to buy.

- **Repeat the process for bridesmaids' dresses.** This time allow for different shapes, styles, and even colors. Make sure the price tags are in line with bridesmaids' personal finances. See "The Ten Commandments (of Not Torturing Your Bridesmaids)" on page 64 for further instructions.

THE CAT WALK, or How to Walk Like a Charm School Graduate

Chances are, you probably have not had much practice walking in a formal gown (not since your high-school prom, anyway). Walking, like breathing, may seem elementary, but there are some pointers we can offer to put the glide in your stride.

- **Above all, choose comfort.** If you shudder at the thought of wearing Carrie Bradshaw's five-inch stilettos, why bother? If you never wear heels, don't start now. Consider comfy ballet slippers, low-heeled sandals, or low pumps. There's a happy medium between Manolos and Aerosoles. Note: the shorter the dress, the more important the shoes.

- **Break 'em in!** You'll be wearing those shoes for at least six or seven hours, so don't just let them gather dust for months before the event. Wear them around the house, and walk up and down stairs. Vacuum or dance in them. One bride we know wore hers out to dinner so she could practice walking and gauge the comfort quotient.

- **My fair lady.** Walk with a book on your head like Eliza Doolittle—it forces you to stand up straight. Visualize balancing the book on your head as you practice walking down the aisle. It's strangely calming.

- **Lose ten pounds.** You heard us! Stand up straight and prepare to visually lose ten pounds. It's a pretty amazing trick.

- **Adopt a model gait.** Supermodel catwalk know-how goes like this: swivel hips, then place one foot directly in front of the other. Choose a song to practice to in order to get the rhythm right. Hum it in your head as you strut.

BRIDESMAIDS

Unless you're paying, no bridesmaid will be happy about blowing the rent on a dress that she will likely wear once. And the more formal the dress, the less likely she'll be able to morph it into something she can use later. Remember this when you're choosing your wedding style.

An Anti-Bride knows that her best pals may not all be a size 6 and, because of her good manners and respect for her friends, she considers dress styles that look good on everyone. For example, while orange on a redhead might be a disaster, blue, dark green, or black dresses are flattering on most women. Mixing up styles (a sheath for one bridesmaid, a strapless for another, a three-quarter-length sleeve for another) is a great way to address a variety of shapes, sizes, style requirements, and body issues.

THE GROOM

Unlike the bride, the groom and his attendants will probably rent their wedding attire. If renting is not an option (or the offerings aren't up to snuff) consider buying the best black suit he can afford and a gorgeous, over-the-top vintage tie. Vintage tuxedos and suits can also make a great look. Just make sure the tux or suit is not shiny in the seat, and dry clean it before wearing, since dust can cause allergies. One faux pas we cannot forgive is wearing shiny plastic shoes. Instead, go for classy wingtips he can wear again, or black Alden loafers (not with a tux, though).

PARENTS

Once the bride and her bridesmaids have selected their dresses, parents should start shopping for their clothes. Make sure your parents see photos of your dress and your bridesmaids' dresses (or the real thing), and give them a clear picture of the style and formality of the wedding. Because they have decades of style savvy on you, trust in your parents' ability to dress themselves correctly (even if your mom has to remind your dad that his tux might need letting out).

Stress Saver. If you plan on taking the traditional route, don't wait around. You'll need to start shopping for your gown at least six months in advance. Grooms should start doing their homework two to three months in advance.

Hip Tip. If you are having a semiformal wedding and want your bridesmaids to be able to wear their dresses again, have them each choose a black, dressy knee-length dress and black strappy high-heeled sandals. Unify the look with a piece of jewelry you have made for them. Your pals will look stunning in dresses that they'll really wear again. Best of all, they will be comfortable and happy, which makes for great photos and a great party atmosphere.

Sticky Situations

Sometimes not knowing what to wear can be so much more harrowing than not knowing what to say! Here is a collection of narrowly missed fashion faux pas, vendor blunders, and solutions.

You're having an island wedding and you aren't sure about the proper level of formality.

Solution: Island weddings are becoming more popular, and style issues are open to interpretation. If you'd like to aim for comfortable, cost effective, and casual, go for it! Remember, if you are wearing a heavy silk gown, and your bridesmaids are easy and breezy in Lilly Pulitzer sundresses and colored beads, there might be a fashion disconnect. Imagine wilting in heavy damask at your Jamaican nuptials while your colorful-sundress-clad bridesmaids do the Watusi with a mai tai in hand, and you'll understand what we mean.

One of your attendants is a man and you're not sure what he should wear.

Solution: Obviously, your male attendant won't be prancing around in a Vera Wang. Usually, he'll wear the same attire as the other male attendants in the wedding party. He can be given an accessory that's different from those of the other male attendants, though, such as a cummerbund, vest, tie, or boutonniere that coordinates with the bridesmaids' attire.

Your seamstress has created a dress that you don't remember approving.

Solution: Unearth the original drawings, photos, and notes on your inspiration for the dress. If a preliminary muslin version was made, go back to it and see how the final product deviates from it. Be honest with yourself: have you gained weight, been body building, or had a breast enhancement? Are you expecting a little one? Remarkably, some women undergo these body-changing experiences but don't understand why the dress doesn't fit the way they remembered. Tactfully and calmly tell your seamstress that the finished product isn't going to work for you, and collaborate with her to find a way to get it back on track. In the worst case, if it's unfixable, forfeit your deposit, retain an attorney, and start shopping, *pronto*.

Your mother wants you to wear her pearls, but your jewelry-designer friend has whipped up a choker using a vintage brooch and semiprecious stones that's runway fabulous.

Solution: A simple dress with a plain strand of pearls is lovely, but it may also be forgettable. On the other hand, if you have a gorgeous piece of jewelry that will be the focal point of your look, you've probably designed or chosen your dress specifically to showcase it. Try a compromise: Wrap the pearls around your wrist or see how the pearls look incorporated with your choker. See if the pearls can be woven into your hairdo. If the above aren't possible, tell your mother you plan to tuck the pearls into a special pocket inside your dress and wear them close to your heart as you walk down the aisle. Then, when you change into your "getaway" outfit, you can wear her pearls proudly.

Your mom wants you to wear her gown, a stiff, yellowed, lace-encrusted relic.

Solution: You can't imagine even pulling it over your head, much less wearing it on the most important day of your life. But, like most things sentimental, it's best that you handle the situation (and her feelings) with care. Tell her that you're honored that she wants you to wear her wedding dress, but let her know that you already have a style in mind that would better suit your figure and make your day perfect (and unfortunately her dress just doesn't fit in with your plan). If her headpiece, her veil, or a piece of her jewelry might complement your gown, ask her if you can wear it. In a nutshell, express how much you appreciate the offer and hope that she understands.

CHAPTER 7

PRE-WEDDING CELEBRATIONS & SHOWERS

If there is one thing we can love, honor, and obey, it's the Anti-Bride's ability to plan an event that's as sparkly as her vintage earrings, but also kick off her pumps and have an icy martini with her people at the drop of a hat (or tiara). Pre-parties are a surefire way to bring disparate groups together to create a cohesive vibe before W-day.

Tight urban tribes tend to cluster together at any social function. You've been at weddings where there's a college dorm table, a metro-fabulous table, a gay and groovy table, a cousins from Kansas table, and a new parents table. Short of issuing everyone team shirts, we advocate creating a mix to promote interesting conversation. Pre-wedding events can serve as clique busters, successfully blending the people in your life and his. Best of all, since most of the parties are held in your honor, all you need to do is throw on a glamorous garment, sip a snappy cocktail, and hang out with your best pals and family—without lifting a finger.

Because you're an Anti-Bride, you don't do the cookie-cutter routine in any aspect of your life, but you still want to protect your friends' and relatives' feelings. In order to do things your own way without offending anyone, you'll need to first gather information about all of the many pre-wedding parties and the traditions that go with them. Use this chapter to learn what's in store and pick up ways to gently guide your family and attendants in the right direction—yours. So if you're not too keen on penis piñatas, strippers, or drunken evenings spent in a white limo, and afternoon tea is a little too grandmotherly for you, look here for the appropriate way to suggest an alternative that better suits your cool style.

The Golden Rules

As long as there have been weddings, there have been pre-parties. These rituals are all a part of the windup to the big day. Below are some of the events you can expect. None is mandatory, so join in where appropriate (for you).

Pre-Wedding Festivities: THE TRADITION

EVENT	PURPOSE
Engagement party	To announce the engagement and allow the bride's and groom's families to meet each other
Bridal shower	To honor the bride and "shower" her with gifts
Bridesmaids' luncheon	To thank the attendants for all of their hard work
Bachelorette party	One last night on the town with the girls before the wedding
Rehearsal dinner	To allow the wedding party and families to get acquainted

HOSTED BY	WHEN
Bride's parents	Shortly after the couple gets engaged and before the formal written announcement is made
Maid of honor, bridesmaids, and sometimes friends or co-workers	At least one month before the wedding (but generally no more than six months)
Bride	One to two weeks before the wedding day
Maid of honor and bridesmaids	The same night as the bachelor party; never the night before the wedding
Groom's parents	The night before the wedding, after the rehearsal of the ceremony, usually ending before midnight

ENGAGEMENT PARTY

The engagement party is usually hosted by the bride's parents. Engagement parties (less popular now than they were in previous decades) serve as a great way for close friends and family members on both sides to get acquainted. This celebration also marks the starting point of the wedding planning and provides a fun setting in which the attendants can meet each other and plot the weeks and months ahead.

Because of the traditional pecking order governing which people are told the big news first, the party should be held after you have told your parents and extended families, but before any newspaper announcement is published. Gift giving is not expected, although small tokens are sometimes given on the sly. Since some brides and grooms use the engagement party as an opportunity to introduce their respective parents, it's important to make the event as low stress as possible; we suggest a simple picnic or an at-home dress-up party with cocktails and hors d'oeuvres.

BRIDAL SHOWER

Originally, the purpose of a bridal shower was to give the new couple a jumpstart on collecting household items they might need when they begin their new life together. Nowadays, most of us are well versed in Williams-Sonoma kitchen chic, and we probably have most of what we need already. So what started off as

I'M PLEASED TO ANNOUNCE . . . ENGAGEMENT PARTY TIDBITS

- *The formal announcement is often made in a toast by the father of the bride-to-be. The groom traditionally follows with a toast of his own to his future bride and her family.*

- *Before the engagement party, the groom's parents are expected to introduce themselves to the bride's parents.*

- *While the parents of the bride traditionally host the engagement party (and they should be given the first opportunity), anyone can throw a party in the couple's honor (except, of course, the couple themselves).*

a utilitarian idea has evolved into an excuse to celebrate, which is fine with us! Traditionally, the maid of honor and the bridesmaids (never the bride's mother or future mother-in-law) host the shower, inviting only female guests. The main activities usually revolve around consumables: food, drinks, and gifts.

Party games are only to be endured. The point of a bridal soiree is to mix the bride's friends and female family members and honor the bride. If it's a couple's shower, the point is to mix the tribes and honor the union. As for what's proper behavior, let's just say you should avoid things like penis piñatas, having "sex toy" showers, or asking sexually suggestive questions of the bride, especially if the bride's mother, grandmother, or mother-in-law happen to attend.

Since the focus of the shower is on gift giving, which is in itself a sensitive subject, a few rules of etiquette govern this celebration:

ETIQUETTE

- Although the bride should not mention her gift registry unless asked, the shower hostess may mention the registry in the shower invitation.

- Shower guests should *never* be asked to help pay for the shower. One shower guest was mortified when, after a lovely lunch at a four-star restaurant, the mother of the bride—who should not have been hosting the shower in the first place—informed everyone at the table what they owed, including the cost of the bride's lunch.

- Guests who are invited to the shower must be invited to the wedding.

BRIDESMAIDS' LUNCHEON

The bridesmaids' luncheon is hosted by the bride for her best pals as a great big thank-you for their efforts. The party can be held as a lunch, which is the norm, a brunch, dinner, or happy hour get-together at a local lounge.

BACHELORETTE PARTY

Squealing girls and strip clubs full of dancing, oily-chested men with socks stuffed in their banana hammocks are becoming a thing of the past. Bonding with your gals is what the bachelorette party is all about, not calling attention to how drunk and tarty you look in public...

THE REHEARSAL DINNER

The rehearsal dinner is a meal following the rehearsal (the walk-through of the wedding) and is often held at a restaurant or at the groom's parents' home. The guest list is limited in order to give the bride and groom an opportunity to spend time with their closest friends and get acquainted with their new family members. Some families might invite all out-of-town guests, especially if the event is a casual backyard barbecue. Most of the time the guest list includes only the bride and groom, their parents, the wedding party (and their spouses or significant others), and the officiant. A quick itinerary sent to all guests should swiftly address any questions about the rehearsal dinner guest list (sometimes out-of-town guests assume they'll be invited to the dinner).

Introducing the cast of characters (and maybe unearthing childhood photos of the bride and groom) is the main function of the rehearsal dinner. Toasts are also typically involved: first the best man, then the groom's father (as host), next the bride and groom (giving thanks to the parents), and finally any other guests. The rehearsal dinner is also the customary time for the bride to present attendants and parents with thank-you gifts.

OH, BEHAVE! If multiple friends approach you about throwing a shower, encourage collaboration—it looks self-serving to have more than one or two. One bride we talked to had seven showers in her honor (one family, one work, and five friend showers, including one couples shower), and the same circle of friends was invited to all but the family and work parties. When asked why she didn't step in to halt the insanity, she replied, "I would never say no to a friend who wants to honor me with a shower." Little did she know the impact it had on those closest to her, and how it made her look—greedy and self-important.

New Rules of the Road

There's nothing set in stone in the pre-party department, but the key for the Anti-Bride is to make them her own. If you'd rather listen to cool jazz at a hot club with your gals than do tequila shots at a strip bar for your bachelorette shindig, make your desires known. If you can't imagine having a high-brow rehearsal dinner at a private club, why not throw a relaxed potluck in your parents' backyard?

Pre-Wedding Festivities: FORGING YOUR OWN PATH

THE TWIST	TWISTING WITHOUT TRAUMA
Can't imagine a boring, sit-down dinner in the banquet room of your local steakhouse? Host your engagement party somewhere innovative—a salsa club, a dance studio, or the beach.	Your town might have a Cuban social club, or Latin American cultural center; see if you can hire the best salsa band and dance teacher to give everyone lessons, and have frosty mojitos ready for the danced-out. Or rent out an Arthur Murray Dance Studio and teach everyone to tango; serve martinis and hors d'oeuvres when the dancing is done. Or wrangle up two surf instructors, rent wetsuits and foam boards, and hit the beach; follow with a bonfire and picnic.
THE TWIST	**TWISTING WITHOUT TRAUMA**
Have a coed shower.	This is an easy, inclusive, and fun twist on pre-wedding party traditions. Instead of segregating the girls from the guys, bring them all together for a cool cocktail party, with gifts, of course.
THE TWIST	**TWISTING WITHOUT TRAUMA**
Make your bridesmaids' "luncheon" a party they'll thank *you* for.	Like the rehearsal dinner, the bridesmaids' luncheon (or party) is the perfect opportunity to give your girls (and guys, if applicable) tokens of your appreciation and love. Anti-Brides say that if you are going to do something nice, make it count. Whether you give them a day of wine tasting, a spa experience, or dinner at a luxe restaurant (but no take-out pizzas, unless Jamie Oliver is making them), show your attendants the love.

THE TWIST	TWISTING WITHOUT TRAUMA
Suggest a tasteful, sophisticated bachelorette party.	Bachelorette parties, often embarrassing spectacles of debauchery, are a development of the last few decades. Do you want yours to resemble an episode of *Girls Behaving Badly,* or do you want it to be a grown-up gathering of sassy, stylish gals with chutzpah, a little cash, and a lot of dash? The de rigueur white limo, seedy strip bar, and cocktails with names like "Sex on the Beach" are *over.*

Because Anti-Brides aim higher, it's your job to gently communicate this to your girls (who are planning the event). How about an evening at your favorite restaurant, a cozy potluck, or an evening of upscale hors d'oeuvres and libations at a wood-lined martini emporium? Another option: hunt down the next Wolfgang Puck at the local culinary school, and hire him to strut his stuff (in the kitchen) on his night off. Even a simple trip to a local bar for an impromptu ladies' night can be fun (just make sure it's at least a week before the wedding). There's no need to spend big bucks or stay out all night. |

THE TWIST	TWISTING WITHOUT TRAUMA
A festive, relaxed rehearsal dinner that helps break the ice.	Peri Wolfman, Williams-Sonoma tastemaker and hosting guru, remembers a clambake she threw in Florida. "I bought pails, shovels, and had wine in buckets and votives in jars." Keeping it fun and low-key makes it easier for people to talk and get to know each other (which, in our eyes, is the key to success).

Hip Tip. To read about showers that ran cold (and to get a bridal-shower eye opener), just log on to the kvetch section of www.Indiebride.com, or www.theKnot.com Web site. They're packed with bridezilla moments and sticky situations.

Sticky Situations

The sheer number of pre-wedding celebrations, each with its own set of preconceived traditions and rituals, can make for a host of uncomfortable circumstances. Read on for advice on how to handle difficult situations.

A friend has approached you about throwing you a bridal shower for your encore wedding, but you don't want to look greedy.

Solution: If this is the second time around for both of you—that is, if you're renewing your vows—it's a little redundant to do a shower with gifts. If you're marrying again to another person, it's a judgment call. If you want to bring good friends together, then have a party. Just don't call it a shower (read: gift fishing).

You want to invite people to the shower whom you can't invite to the wedding.

Solution: For shame! The only exception is a shower hosted by office co-workers, who might give you a quickie shower at work to wish you well. If you wish, you might consider hosting a gathering after the honeymoon, inviting those who didn't make the cut.

The groom's parents are divorced—who hosts the rehearsal dinner?

Solution: The first option, the best-case scenario, is that the groom's parents are on speaking terms and are willing to cohost and split expenses. The second option is for the groom to speak to his parents separately to see who would like to finance and host the event, and then let the other parent know that he or she will be an honored guest. The third option is for him to speak to his parents, telling them that you plan to pay for the dinner yourselves and encouraging them to "host" in any way that seems comfortable to them. The idea is to celebrate your marriage, not create more conflict; try to communicate this to the stubborn minded.

You'd like to exclude a problem sibling from the pre-wedding festivities altogether.

Solution: Excluding anyone will cause serious, never-to-be-forgotten conflicts in your family, so weigh the pros and cons carefully. If you do decide to exclude the problem sibling, put on your PR hat and remember, as you're excluding him or her, to say and do only those things that will put you both in the best light possible. As with most tricky situations, open communication is the key. Sit down with the sibling and your parents and openly discuss the reasons for your decision. Lori Leibovich of www.Indiebride.com

says, "Reiterate that the sibling is an important member of the family but you have concerns about his or her behavior, then lay out your concerns. Try not to put him or her on the defensive, though." Having witnesses to the interaction, namely your parents, can help prevent "he said/she said" situations. If it's in your heart, give your sibling a chance, since excluding him or her from any part of your wedding shuts a door permanently.

Your fiancé's mother wants to come to your bachelorette party.

Solution: Your "hip and groovy" mother-in-law may have a problem with boundaries. And if she attends, you will have a problem when your girlfriends start reminiscing about your pre-wedding days, before her darling boy came into your life. Since your compatriots can recount the details of your sexual history with the precision of forensic pathologists (the details becoming more elaborate with each subsequent libation), it's best if the mother-in-law isn't included. What to do? Go out to dinner as a group, and also invite your own mother or your favorite aunt, enlisting her help. After dinner, your mom or aunt simply says to your mother-in-law, "OK, Martha, let's get going so these kids can have some real fun." Works like a charm (from www.Indiebride.com).

Your maid of honor is hell-bent on getting the royal treatment.

Solution: So the maid of honor is pushing for a bachelorette weekend at a Napa Valley spa as your cash-strapped bridesmaids cringe? While it's not your job to plan your own party, you can reel in the maid of honor and let her know you want something simple—nothing too over the top. If she insists, then the two of you can go dutch on a spa weekend, and do something lo-fi with the rest of the girls.

Hip Tip. The number one question discussed by bridesmaids on Internet wedding message boards is "When did bachelorette parties turn into mini-vacations, and how am I supposed to afford one?" Be aware of the cost of your wedding events and how it impacts others.

CHAPTER 8

PLANNING & EXECUTION—
The Ceremony

Just watch—you flash that engagement ring, and suddenly everyone's a wedding planner. As soon as you set a date, people will start ankle biting, whether it's about a conflict with your sister Sally's graduation (same weekend), your cousin Tina's wedding (the weekend before), or your best friend's nonrefundable Barbados vacation, coincidentally scheduled for the second weekend in May.

Close your eyes, breathe deeply, and count to ten.

If you have the luxury of time, your wedding space is available on a different weekend, and the thought of not having your best friend there with you gives you an anxiety attack, then reschedule. Otherwise, let it be known that this is your day and, while you'll do your best to make sure that all the main players are included, you aren't a miracle worker. You have enough on your plate. Your main focus at this point should be to decide when, where, who, how many, how much, and "how do I look?"

Once you have a good idea of where this is heading, involve the families, but be prepared for push-back, especially if you're coming from different cultural or religious backgrounds or the families live in different parts of the country. Think like a CEO: write a mission statement outlining what your event is all about and how you want to stage it. We have talked to too many brides who have stated flat out that their wedding was one big compromise. *To thine own self be true.*

To get the most out of your resources and plan the ceremony you want, you need insider information. This chapter will help you manage the logistics that surface when you're planning and implementing your wedding ceremony, and *it will* help you identify and steer clear of the etiquette landmines along the way before you step on one.

The Golden Rules

Planning: THE TRADITION

Historically, the bride's family has always called the shots from a planning stand-point, mainly because they were footing the bill.

Deciding when to hold your nuptials often involves balancing what's best for your guests and getting the best rates for your budget. No etiquette rules govern when to have a wedding, but here are some guidelines that will ensure that the majority of A-listers attend. When determining the date, it's customary to consider the following:

- **The day of the week:** Sure, it's cheaper to have a wedding on a Friday, but if you want most of your invitees to come, it's best to hold it on the most popular day for weddings, which happens to be Saturday.

- **Religious holidays:** Avoid Christmas and Easter. Travel costs are higher, and most people would rather be with their families than at someone's wedding.

- **Nonreligious holidays:** Steer clear of holidays like Thanksgiving (and the Saturday that follows), Memorial Day, Labor Day, Martin Luther King Jr. Day, and the Fourth of July. These coveted days off are also known as the workin' stiffs' mini-breaks.

- **American sentimental days:** Valentine's Day, Mother's Day, and Father's Day are off limits, too. Fathers, mothers, and lovers deserve to be honored on their days, not attend yours.

- **School and summer vacations:** "Dude! Like, don't make me spend spring break in a tux! I'm totally in Cabo with my bros." Check with people on your A list before booking a date during spring and summer. Find out when college-age students (especially your little brother) will be on break as well.

- **Winter months:** Ice storms, canceled flights, blizzards, and acts of God can ruin your idealized winter wonderland. An Anna Karenina snow-princess fantasy can turn into a snowbound horror show if you book anytime between Christmas and the beginning of March, depending on your location. Work within the safety months: March through November.

Now comes the issue of ceremony location and type. The time-honored, traditional wedding is, of course, a religious ceremony in a house of worship. In certain circumstances, a civil ceremony at city hall or the office of a justice of the peace has also been considered acceptable. If you decide to go ultra traditional and have a wedding in a house of worship—and we're not saying there's anything wrong with that—know that you need to follow their rules. Think attending multiple premarital counseling sessions with a priest is only for true believers or that your rabbi was joking when he said you needed to cover your arms in the temple? Guess again. Wearing attire that the church rules say is inappropriate or not completing pre-wedding requirements will give your officiant reason to stop your wedding before it begins. As soon as you get engaged, be sure to contact your house of worship to find out about any expectations they have for you.

Execution: THE TRADITION

So you've familiarized yourself with the traditions and commonsense guidelines involved in planning your event, but now you're wondering what rules govern the ceremony itself. Do we have to use a prewritten ceremony? Where does everyone stand, and in what order do they walk in and out? Who sits where? Believe it or not, the positioning of the wedding party can vary from one religion to another.

PROCESSIONAL: WHO GOES WHERE?

For a formal Christian wedding:

- Groom, the best man, and the officiant stand in front of the altar.

- The processional order goes like this: the groomsmen (one at a time), the bridesmaids (also one at a time), the maid of honor, the ring bearer, the flower girl, and finally the bride on the right arm of whoever is giving her away.

For a formal Jewish wedding:

- The processional order goes like this: the rabbi, the bride's grandparents, the groom's grandparents, the ushers in pairs, the best man, the groom on his father's right and mother's left, the bridesmaids individually, the maid of honor, the ring bearer, the flower girl, and finally the bride on her father's right arm and mother's left.

RECESSIONAL

When all the vows have been said, the rings have been exchanged, the couple has kissed, and it's time to hit the reception, the bridal party will make its way down the aisle in traditional wedding style.

For a formal Christian wedding: In pairs, the bride holds the groom's right arm, the flower girl walks with the ring bearer, the maid of honor walks with the best man, and the bridesmaids walk with the ushers.

For a formal Jewish wedding: The bride holds the groom's left arm, the bride's parents walk together, the groom's parents walk together, the flower girl walks with the ring bearer, the maid of honor walks with the best man, the ushers walk with the bridesmaids, and the cantor walks with the rabbi.

GUEST SEATING

During a Christian ceremony, the bride's family usually sits on the left, and the groom's family sits on the right (it's the opposite for Jewish ceremonies). Parents sit in the front row, and both sets of grandparents and other relatives sit directly behind them. If you're dealing with divorced parents, Mom (and her new husband or wife, if she has one) sits in the front row, and Dad (and his wife or husband) sits directly behind your other relatives.

THE CEREMONY SCRIPT

Because a marriage is a legal contract between partners, wedding ceremonies tend to include standard, prewritten language, partly to ensure that everyone understands what's being promised. The traditional American ceremony is a script containing a statement of intention to marry, vows, exchange of rings, and a kiss to seal the deal. Depending on your faith, the prewritten ceremony required by your house of worship may also involve readings, songs, prayers, and other rituals. However, you may be able to choose some of the readings, songs, and other elements.

New Rules of the Road

Planning: FORGING YOUR OWN PATH

Weddings are no longer paid for entirely by the bride's father, and we all know that the dowry is a sexist and antiquated notion. Modern weddings are often funded collectively by the bride's and groom's families and the couple themselves. But with this shared financial responsibility come new stakeholders. Everyone who writes a check may want to weigh in on the decisions. At the end of the day, it's the bride and groom who call the shots. So, while you may want to adhere to certain meaningful traditions, feel free to do things your own way, if it will make your wedding special to you and your groom. Below are some twists on tradition that you can use to make your ceremony truly yours.

THE TWIST	TWISTING WITHOUT TRAUMA
Have a nondenominational wedding	While church weddings are common, not everyone's religious or cultural beliefs match up. If you're not religious, you don't want to deal with the rules and regulations that churches impose, or you don't want to choose between your two religions, consider holding the wedding at a nondenominational church or chapel. If you and your mate aren't interested in premarital counseling every Saturday morning for the next four months but you still want to have a church wedding, find a rentable nondenominational church (and spend your Saturdays sinning, not saving your souls).
Plan a civil ceremony with personality	Having a civil ceremony doesn't have to be like renewing your driver's license at the DMV. You can have a civil ceremony at any location, from a nondenominational chapel to an outdoor park or a museum. Ceremonies performed by a justice of the peace, county clerk, judge, mayor, or governor are perfectly appropriate. A civil ceremony allows leeway for wedding style, vows, and location. It's often a great alternative for multifaith, multicultural, or same-sex couples who want something special without the stress that organized religion can add.

THE REHEARSAL

Usually held a day before the wedding, the rehearsal is a walk-through of the ceremony. The officiant or wedding coordinator is the conductor of the rehearsal—he knows the ropes, so follow his lead. He will instruct your wedding party how to form the procession and recession, walk up and down the aisle, and where to stand. Vows, readings, and prayers aren't spoken, so the rehearsal is short and sweet.

COMMITMENT CEREMONIES

Marianne Puechl of the Rainbow Wedding Network says that while many gay ceremonies lean toward tradition, one of the main hurdles for couples is finding gay-friendly vendors. You might imagine that in this day and age (not to mention economy) vendors would lighten up about what they consider to be "normal and appropriate." But this isn't always the case. Consider the lesbian couple trying to rent a tuxedo for their wedding—where do they go? A traditional men's shop probably wouldn't have her size and the whole experience would make her feel uncomfortable. Dealing with these challenges (that your straight sisters never face) becomes easier when you reinterpret standard traditions and create new ones just for you. For example, find a gay-friendly seamstress who is quick with the needle and skilled in the art of feminine bespoke apparel. At the end of the day, money is green, you're in love, and you deserve quality, attention, and respect. Anyone who treats you otherwise is not worthy of your patronage.

Stress Saver. Check out www.pridebride.com, www.twobrides.com, and www.rainbowweddingnetwork.com for lists of vendors who know how to behave, venues, and other resources, including wedding consulting, gift registries, gay-friendly honeymoon packages, and even gay-friendly realtors.

OH, BEHAVE! Seeing a rainbow flag draped over the gift table may be fine for your grandmother, but a glimpse of you in a tuxedo and a buzz cut may send her to the emergency room, especially if she's never seen you in your butch garb. Keep in mind that some of your family members may think of you as you used to be, not as the cool and groovy person you are now. Find a happy medium between your true style and sheer shock value.

SHOTGUN WEDDING

If you only have weeks to plan your nuptials, whether it's because of pending military service or pregnancy (or because you're in a state of passion hotter than a pepper sprout), good manners are still a part of the equation. Need to get married in three weeks? Send out your invitations immediately. (You could have a one-night "invitation bee," where your bridesmaids and relatives divide up the guest list, write out invitations, and help call or e-mail guests.) Just make sure your guests have at least two weeks' notice. To keep your sanity and stay on schedule, be realistic about what can be done in that short time frame. Pick one or two things that are important to you and lose the rest.

Stress Saver. Civil ceremonies are ideal if you're in a time crunch since they can be arranged within a few days. A quickie wedding on your lunch break will allow you to focus on planning your reception.

DESTINATION WEDDING

Destination weddings are becoming increasingly popular; some say it's because we've become more nomadic and don't have the same sense of "roots" that our forefathers did. Whatever! Having a wedding in an exotic locale is a hoot! The upside? You can keep it small. The people in your vast, spread-out network—cousins, friends, co-workers, your mom's high school chums, and your father's old college buddies—don't need to devote an entire weekend to your wedding. Crys Stewart of *WeddingBells* suggests having a ceremony of blessing when you return, to soothe any hurt feelings among family members. Here's what you do: Go to Bali (alone! or with your best people), have a blast, and hop on a plane home, looking gorgeous and tanned, feeling happy and relaxed. Then have the blessing ceremony, at a church or any place you want. Generally, the bride and groom (already married) walk down the aisle arm in arm. Skip the white dress, bridal party, and bouquet—just wear something fabulous and you are ready to rumble. Then throw a party for all of your well-wishers and have a blast.

Hip Tip. To find clergy that perform interfaith ceremonies, check out www.weddingofficiants.com or www.interfaith.org for more sources.

ELOPE NOW, PARTY LATER

If you decide to sneak out of town, and have a private ceremony with just the two of you or immediate family, throw a party for everyone who wasn't at the ceremony when you return. This strategy also works well for couples who decide to get married while living overseas and find it impractical to invite all the cousins and work buddies.

Carolyn and Laurent celebrated their nuptials alone and, after announcing their marriage, had three dress-up cocktail parties: one in the Washington D.C. area, where Carolyn's family and college buddies live; one in San Francisco, where Carolyn, Laurent, and their urban tribe live; and one in Paris, where Laurent's family lives. This was a better option than having one big event, which would have involved lots of travel time for many dear family members and friends (some of whom had small children).

Execution: FORGING YOUR OWN PATH

You want to adhere to proper etiquette, but you want your wedding to express your relationship, personality, lifestyle, and beliefs. There's no need to have a standard wedding just because you want to do things "right." We know couples who have wedded in a wooded grove, atop a mountain, and at a racetrack, accompanied by everything from a rockabilly band to a 1980s new-wave group.

Hip Tip. If you want certain beloved people at the wedding, check with them before you choose an exotic locale. They want to see you walk down the aisle, but Costa Rica might be a stretch for your seventy-five-year-old granny.

MAKING THE CEREMONY MORE PERSONAL

Here are some specific ways to make your wedding ceremony your own:

- If you're marrying in a house of worship, reverse positions with the officiant so you're facing your guests.

- At a small wedding, have the guests surround you in a circle or semicircle.

- Follow the Asian custom of standing outside the house of worship and greeting guests as they arrive.

- Have ushers hand candles to guests as they enter the house of worship. Start by lighting one guest's candle, and then have that guest light the candle of the person next to him, who in turn lights the candle of the person next to him, continuing until all the candles are lit.

- Investigate traditions from your ethnic background and incorporate those that are meaningful to you, such as jumping the broom, or passing a lighted candle.

VOW-WRITING CLINIC (SAYING IT THE WRITE WAY)

You may choose to steer clear of the standard wedding vows ("love," yes, "honor," yes, but "obey?") and write your own. Let your officiant guide you initially. Some guidelines:

- Keep it short and sweet. No twenty-minute monologues describing every step in your relationship from day one. Boring.

- Keep it positive. Don't refer to any previous breakups or make ups that have taken place along your winding path toward marriage. It's not a made-for-TV movie; it's your wedding.

- Write your vows on index cards in case you blank. Many people do.

- Check with the officiant to make sure the wording doesn't conflict with the church's beliefs (lest they shut you down).

OH, BEHAVE! If you decide to elope or have a small wedding, send out announcements after the fact announcing the big news and the upcoming party to celebrate.

Hip Tip. If you rent a public site, find out whether you need a permit. A surprise visit from a park ranger instructing you and your guests to evacuate the premises mid-ceremony would be high on our list of etiquette violations.

Sticky Situations

Maybe you and your fiancé need to get away from the pressure of planning, and worlds (or religions) might collide. Or maybe you and your sweetie are from different sides of the track. Whatever your situation, we've got the answers for you.

You eloped, and your friends and family feel cheated. What to do?

Solution: Carolyn and Laurent kept their wedding a secret from everyone (including friends) for months. They just wanted a little peace and quiet until they were ready to plan their events. When the time is right for both of you, tell your family and friends (together or individually) about the nuptials, and explain your reasons for doing it on your own (e.g., you needed privacy, peace, or whatever). Then throw a big party where everyone gets together and celebrates your union, and they'll feel like they shared in the moment with you.

You and your significant other want to have an interfaith wedding, but you don't know how to make it happen.

Solution: You could incorporate both faiths into the service, pick one over the other, or opt for a civil ceremony. One bride found the only rabbi and Catholic priest in Maryland willing to perform a joint Catholic and Jewish ceremony. The ceremony was in Hebrew and English and was held at a university chapel. Another couple chose to have a Catholic ceremony since her fiancé didn't practice any religion—but both had to attend premarital classes and promise that their children would be raised Catholic. If you can't decide or the process becomes too taxing, you can always opt for a civil ceremony. No matter what you choose, expect your families to push back. Try to anticipate possible arguments and come up with solutions to help them feel included. Be prepared to simply explain (and stand by) your decision, and hope they understand.

You're having an interfaith wedding and family members can't accept it.

Solution: First, reassure your family that you love your religion and that you're not turning your back on everything they've taught you. Tell them the door is open for discussion, and you welcome hearing anything that's on their mind. Communicate how important it is to you that they remain a part of your wedding. Listen to them and allow them input, but follow your heart and act according to your comfort level when deciding your course of action.

You want to have the ceremony and reception in the same room (or garden).

Solution: There's no etiquette rule that says the ceremony and reception have to be held in different locations. We suggest serving a buffet (it's easier to manage and usually less expensive), which can be set up in advance and hidden behind folding screens. Conduct the wedding ceremony in front of the screens, with your guests sitting at tables, then have your photos taken with your wedding party in a predetermined spot at the other end of the room (in full view of all). During this time, the screens come down and the space transforms from ceremony to reception site. Although it's not the norm, more couples are choosing to seat their guests at tables for the ceremony when the two events need to be held in the same space. If you can, you might instead have the ceremony outside or in another part of the facility and then come into the reception room to celebrate.

The number of guests on the bride's side is significantly larger than the groom's, but you don't want one side of the church to be packed while the other is nearly empty.

Solution: When couples get married in one partner's hometown and the other partner's family needs to travel some distance to attend, this situation is common. It's perfectly fine to populate the groom's side with the bride's people. It will look more balanced as a result, which will improve the ambiance of the ceremony.

Your divorced parents dislike each other and you're not sure where to seat them.

Solution: Traditional etiquette gurus would tell you to put them together on the bride's side of the church, and at the reception seat them as far away from each other as possible. We say, if they're uncomfortable sitting close to each other, have an usher seat them in separate rows on the bride's side, or even allow them to choose their seats. During the reception, if you're going for assigned seating, have them sit as far away from each other as needed. Enlist a sibling or cousin to perform peace-keeping duties if necessary, and make sure supportive loved ones are posted at each table.

You want your divorced parents, who can't stand each other, to walk you down the aisle.

Solution: Well, isn't it about time Mom and Dad acted like adults and rose above their animosity at least for one day? Talk to them individually. If they can't do this one thing for you, then neither of them should walk you down. In that event, we suggest choosing another relative, sibling, or friend, or walking yourself down the aisle.

You're having trouble deciding which of your two dads, real or step, should walk you down the aisle.

Solution: Who says you have to choose? While traditional etiquette would tell you that your "real" dad should do the job, there's no reason that you shouldn't be "given away" by the person nearest and dearest to you: your dad, mom, uncle, brother, or best pal. Why not walk down the aisle with a dad on each arm? Do what's comfortable and know that whatever your gut tells you is the best scenario.

It's your second marriage—who walks you down the aisle?

Solution: Again, our view is that whoever holds an important place in your life should walk with you—your groom, your children, your father, your best friend.

CHAPTER 9

PLANNING & EXECUTION—
The Reception

You've already done most of the hard work—you've created a budget, sent out the invitations, ordered your dress, hired a caterer, and rented your space. Now for the fun part: implementing your wedding style, planning the menu, decorating the reception site, and choosing the music. Making it fabulous and staying true to your voice, look, and community is what your event is all about. Use this chapter as a guide to handling the specific issues, value judgments, looks, moods, and ideas that are associated with planning the party of a lifetime. We implore you not to deluge yourself with wedding magazines. You'll end up needing a chiropractic adjustment from just carrying them around and find yourself with information overload. This is counterproductive to your mission: celebrating your union by having an event that uniquely reflects your style (within your budget) and includes the people that make your life stellar.

The Golden Rules

You might have a beach blanket bonfire, a salsa-infused soiree, or a sit-down at the Savoy! Whatever your pleasure, be assured that we've got you covered on the myriad of etiquette questions that arise (but we wouldn't dare tell you which fork to use!).

Table Manners: THE TRADITION

Depending on your wedding style, reception food can be anything from a barbecue in a rented barn to filet mignon at a five-star hotel. There are many ways to present your tasty tidbits—below are the traditional scenarios.

THE SIT-DOWN

A sit-down meal is the easiest way to say "elegant" (read: spare no expense). Begin with a cocktail hour. Hors d'oeuvres are typically passed by waitstaff rather than set out on a buffet table. Offer four kinds of hors d'oeuvres for each hour of the cocktail hour; include one vegetarian appetizer and no more than one shellfish. For the sit-down portion of the meal, stick to three courses. Offering a choice of entrees is nice, but you're not Virgin Atlantic, so you don't need to offer "chicken or beef," although providing a vegetarian option is becoming the standard—you can expect about 10 percent of your guests to choose the non-meat option.

THE BUFFET

Buffets are considered less formal than sit-down meals and can be held any time of day. Passing cold glasses of champagne or a signature drink on a tray is a civilized beginning. Serve the meal on a long table, and have smaller, round tables preset with silverware and name cards for guests. Make sure entree choices have staying power, since the foods will be sitting around for a while, and keep hot foods in chafing dishes to keep them warm. Chef-attended stations (for large cuts of meat like roast beef that are sliced for guests on the spot, or custom pastas where guests can choose sauces) are popular. This option is less expensive than the sit-down since you're not paying as much for the presentation or serving of the food.

A MEAL OF HORS D'OEUVRES

If your wedding falls somewhere between the breakfast, lunch, and dinner hours, you might consider serving hors d'oeuvres only. In this scenario, you might serve two substantial items along with other lighter items. This type of meal can be served buffet style or passed on trays. In either case, offer a variety of hot and cold items,  and serve at least four selections for every hour of the reception. Considering that varied savory hors d'oeuvres (and plenty of 'em) are a little piece of heaven, we'll take hobnobbing, noshing, imbibing, and circulating any day over a sit-down affair.

DESSERT AND CHAMPAGNE

In the days before the dreaded "cake in the face" smashing trend, the wedding cake was a symbol of good luck and fertility. Taste wasn't a concern since guests didn't taste the cake at all, but crumbled it over the bride's head to ensure her fertility. Over the centuries, the tiered cake has evolved into a staple at wedding receptions, and talented cake bakers have created flavors and textures to tempt any palate. At most receptions of any type, the cake-cutting ritual is announced by the best man or toastmaster and is performed after the meal is done and speeches are made. The bride and groom make the first cut and should feed each other a small piece (no cake in the face, please).

At the turn of the century, and into World War II, champagne and cake (or punch and cake) receptions were commonplace. During the war, when milk, butter, and other staples were rationed, family members and neighbors would pool their ration coupons to purchase the requisite ingredients for the wedding cake. Homes, school or church auditoriums, or private clubs served as reception spaces. Today,

OH, BEHAVE! If the plated meal is served as a lunch, offer fewer hors d'oeuvres and make sure they're on the light side.

a champagne and cake reception can be spruced up with a run to Trader Joe's or your local beverage emporium for hors d'oeuvres, cheese, and loaves of crusty French bread. You can still feed the troops without going broke, and people won't suffer from that cake and champagne "sugar buzz."

Seating: THE TRADITION

Typically, the bridal party will sit at a designated central spot aptly named the bridal table. The traditional seating arrangement is as follows: the maid of honor (to the groom's left), best man (to the bride's right), and bridesmaids and ushers on either side. Close relatives should be seated nearest to the bridal table and others farther away. If Mom and Dad are divorced, seat them together if they're on good terms, or far apart if not.

OH, BEHAVE!

It's perfectly proper to ask the caterer for a "wedding basket" to take with you. Chances are you'll be a whirling dervish at your reception and won't have a chance to taste all the treats you so painstakingly chose for your big day. What could be more elegant and romantic than a late-night picnic in your honeymoon suite? Plus you'll need a jolt of energy for what comes next!

New Rules of the Road

Table Manners: FORGING YOUR OWN PATH

As you can see, tradition actually offers plenty of etiquette-approved options for feeding your wedding guests. However, there's no reason you shouldn't add a dash of your own inimitable personality to your menu. Below are a few ideas.

THE TWIST	TWISTING WITHOUT TRAUMA
Incorporate foods representing your or your groom's ethnic heritage in your menu.	Think appetizers: serving spanakopita, caviar, pierogis, or mini gourmet pizzas is a fun way to throw a little Greek, Russian, Polish, or Italian flavor into the proceedings. However, it's best not to make the menu 100 percent ethnic (unless everyone can easily digest curry –and can weather that after-curry aroma that lingers in the air and on clothing hours after it's been served).

THE TWIST	TWISTING WITHOUT TRAUMA
Serve it up local and luxe.	Incorporate some hometown charm: have a Southern cake room, where all the neighbors and family display their finest homemade confections in a designated room at the reception. The best part? Avoid that $3,000 wedding cake bill (priceless). Or do what Rachel, a Cape Cod girl, did: serve up raw seafood in ice-filled vintage rowboats. Classy and homespun, always with flair and good taste.

Hip Tip. When everyone's been seated, the best man stands and makes the first toast, followed by a thank-you toast by the groom and often the bride. The couples' parents toast next, and then other relatives and friends may make their toasts. When others are toasting them, the bride and groom usually stay seated and quietly smile. Etiquette experts differ regarding whether it's proper for them to take a sip at the conclusion of the toast. Guests making toasts should make their speeches short and tasteful (no embarrassing revelations or cutting remarks), and they should be sober (no rambling, drunken monologues!). Additionally, it's not a bad idea for them to talk to the other toastmasters to get an idea of what they're going to say, in order to avoid repeating the same sentiments proffered by previous speakers.

Seating: FORGING YOUR OWN PATH

Despite the importance given to reception seating, there's no need for you to obsess over whom to put where, nor do you need to group generations, families, old college buddies, and urban cliques together. Additionally, you don't have to be the UN protocol director, making sure that every subculture, generation, race, and sexual preference is represented at each table. You want to create a lively, but not forced, mix. And it's only good manners to care about the well-being of the people you entertain. Don't use your social-animal dorm buddy as a catalyst to draw your partially deaf great-aunt and the five Romanian programmers out of their shells. Additionally, don't exile your out-of-towners to social Siberia, or create a college buddy table (sure to be the loudest and rowdiest).

For your single guests, think *opportunity!* Weddings are one of the best ways we know to meet new people from different social circles. It's for this very reason that single bridesmaids have been known to have meltdowns if their gowns are awful. If an older couple is funny and savvy, put them at the urbanites table. But if Aunt Meg is shy and reserved, she might be more comfortable with people of her own generation. Mix it up, but not to the peril of your guests.

RECEPTION RUMBLE

As in a scene out of *West Side Story,* real-life incarnations of the Sharks and the Jets faced off at a recent wedding we attended. The "cooler than you" urban tribe, who were seated together, lurked in a corner, smoking and smirking, as the Gap-clad suburbanites whooped it up on the dance floor to "Celebrate." Each group drew the wagons in tighter while the reception progressed. A better seating plan would have prevented this awkward situation.

Putting Ambiance into the Ordinary

You've got the space. Now what are you going to do with it? Look to your personal tastes and budget, and the event will almost design itself. Julie and Gary are urban bon vivants who embrace an eclectic style. They own a cocktail lounge and an interior design firm, melding Victorian, 1940s, and costume elements in their home and work surroundings. Their mission: to have lo-fi yet luxe parties that combine comfort and style with plenty of wine and hors d'oeuvres. If you think of entertaining as a way of life as opposed to a chore, you can bring together your "best of" elements the way they did: a sumptuous outdoor country bacchanal, with a gourmet potluck spread, claw-footed bathtubs full of Napa wine on ice, and a Moulin Rouge–style wedding gown. Quirky? Yes. Appropriate? Absolutely. Boring? Never

Consider your personal style when choosing your reception décor. Chances are, if you like the clean and classic lines of French brasserie tableware, then hot pink glass plates and black roses would be a little over the top for you. Know thyself, and the appropriate décor will follow (as will the food and the drinks).

The key to planning the perfect event is consistency—everything, from the wedding attire to the decorations, party favors, food, and entertainment, needs to ring true and match up. In art, as in life, be consistent. A 1920s Gatsby-style garden party? Skip the DJ and bubble machine and go for a three-piece jazz ensemble. An eclectic "around the world" multiculti soiree? Pass on the cheese puffs and vegetable platter and go for things like saté, naan bread, and stuffed grape leaves. A country picnic? Lose the satin ball gown and go for a floral sundress. Show consistency, and you'll always be in good taste.

OUTDOOR WET-IQUETTE:

The botanical garden you read about in *Better Homes and Gardens* may seem perfect, but buyer beware—weather issues are always waiting in the wings. You can't count on that perfect October day: a sudden heat wave or a thunderstorm could strike unannounced. For out-door weddings, the best rule of thumb is to plan for the worst. No matter what the weather reports say, rent a tent or have a nearby covered area large enough to hold everyone comfortably, just in case. For ultimate guest comfort, have generators for heating, air-conditioning, and cooking ready for duty.

COMMODE CACHE

With more than one hundred guests at Julie and Gary's at-home wedding, guest gridlock at the WCs would have been an issue if the couple hadn't figured out a solution. They set up a charming and functional outdoor étagère for guest primping outside the jiffy johns by hanging a dividing curtain under a tree for privacy, placing an antique mirror over the wash-basin, and filling mason jars with fresh flowers. A small white iron lattice table set with disposable hand towels provided a place for guests to set their purses for lipstick touchups. Scented candles in ribbon-festooned jars were suspended inside each loo to help dispense trapped air inside. Divine inspiration!

OH, BEHAVE! According to Amy Goodman at *In Style*, centerpieces should not hinder your line of vision. Nothing's worse than a centerpiece that obscures your dining partners.

TIPS ON TABLETOP GLAMOUR

Peri Wolfman, a tabletop guru at Williams-Sonoma, believes wedding ambiance has less to do with "dos and don'ts" than with "yes, and why not?" She knows what works, but she also knows how to bend rules and reinterpret the standard overproduced wedding elements. Easy, breezy, and never fussy, Peri sets the table for us:

- Outside is easier than inside because you can pack little gourmet picnic baskets, light up mason jars with votives, and hand out cool vintage quilts for guests to sit on.

- Always use cloth napkins and real wineglasses. The rest can be paper or plastic.

- Placing wildflowers in old pitchers brings whimsy to the scene.

- Place bottles of champagne and wine in ice-filled metal galvanized tubs, with bottles of microbrew mixed in.

- An indoor event is automatically more formal—you can't use paper or plastic. Simple décor works: try candles and chair covers, which can transform a room (although they can be prohibitively expensive, and people can trip over them). Choose beer in bottles over a keg, and serve a signature cocktail and excellent wine.

DESTINATION EXPECTATION

If you're having a destination wedding, make it worth your guests' while. This means if guests are flying six hours across the country, then driving an hour to your wedding, don't throw a backyard barbecue with a keg of Bud. Jewelry designer Lisa Mackey had this happen to her, and she said it was awful. "I had a vision of something more elegant than dogs and burgers," she says. Our advice: the greater your guests' difficulty factor is, the higher their expectation factor will be. Try to keep your guests' comfort, expense, and ease of travel in mind when you're choosing your destination spot.

Some Traditions We Can Do Without . . .

	Why Do We Do It?	New Rule
RECEIVING LINE	A receiving line, usually formed after the ceremony or during the reception, is one way a bride, groom, and their families get face time with their guests. The line includes the bride's parents, the groom's parents, the happy couple, and the bridal honor attendants.	Since most wedding guests see the receiving line as something akin to standing in line at the grocery store and being forced to make small talk with people they barely know, give the people what they want! Shrimp on a stick and a glass of bubbly. Lose the receiving line, especially if you have more than fifty guests.
GARTER TOSS	Back in fourteenth-century Europe, having a piece of the bride's clothing was good luck. Guests would ruin the bride's dress, frantically ripping off pieces of fabric. To protect themselves from this assault, brides began voluntarily throwing various items to the guests—the garter belt being one of them. When drunk male guests started to try to remove the garter themselves, the men felt it necessary to step in. As a result, the custom evolved, and now the groom removes and tosses the garter.	Skip the garter toss. 
BOUQUET TOSS	Bridal brutality wasn't just performed by the guys. In merry old England, female guests joined in, ripping pieces of the bride's dress and flowers in order to obtain some of her good luck. To escape from the crowd, the bride would toss her bouquet and hightail it out of there. Today, catching the bouquet is considered a sign that you'll be the next to marry.	Don't do the bouquet toss. It's now in vogue for "can't be bothered" gals to run in the opposite direction of the bouquet, the result of which is the bouquet landing with a resounding "thwack" on the floor. To get in front of this new trend, hand your bouquet to your best, unmarried pal for good luck.
THROWING RICE	Rice has long been considered a symbol of fertility and prosperity all over the world. In addition to rice, wheat, figs, dates, coins, dried fruit, and even eggs have traditionally been thrown at the bride and groom.	You don't want anyone in four-inch Manolos to slip and fall on rice while wishing you bon voyage, so if you must have something thrown at you, how about flower petals, confetti, or even birdseed?

Why Do We Do It?	New Rule
INSIPID WEDDING DANCES Group dances like the Macarena, the chicken dance, the electric slide, and the bunny hop allow people with two left feet to get on the dance floor.	Outlaw all ridiculous group dances (and any equally offensive songs), and tar and feather any DJs who consider them crowd-pleasers. Put a clause in your DJ or band contract that prohibits tacky songs and dances, and give the DJ or bandleader a list of songs you don't want.
DOLLAR DANCE This Polish custom has each guest pay to dance with the bride or groom at the reception. The money is intended to help with the honeymoon expenses.	This ritual might have a place in Eastern Europe but not at any wedding we'd attend. Unless you're a daughter of a mob boss, never walk around with a silk pillowcase collecting contributions (or stuff currency of any denomination in your dress).
THE CAKE IN THE FACE SMASH Historically, feeding each other cake symbolized how the couple would "feed and nourish" the relationship forever. Somehow this ritual evolved into smashing cake into each other's faces.	Throughout the reception, the bride and groom must demonstrate respect and love for each other, to start off their marriage successfully. If you'd like to feed each other, do so tenderly. This means no cake up the nose.
BRIDE AND GROOM'S FIRST DANCE The first dance symbolizes the consummation of the wedding vows.	Consummate your vows any way you like, but we prefer the bedroom.
APPOINTING A TOASTMASTER (SOMETIMES THE DJ) He or she acts as master of ceremonies, announcing the arrival of the bridal couple and emceeing the event.	Nix the emcee action. It gives your elegant event a game-show feel.

You know what we mean: that alcoholic uncle who makes a scene at every family function or the friend of a friend who ingratiates his way into your party, invited or not. You don't have to please all of the people all of the time, but there are behaviors that you, the bride, need to avoid altogether with regard to your guests. Here are some examples of common pitfalls—view them and take a vow to avoid them.

ETIQUETTE DON'T	STRATEGY
Not providing adequate directions to festivities	Drive the MapQuest directions yourself to see if they really work. Then make corrections to them. Make sure to include a few phone numbers so guests can call if they get lost.
Having a cash bar at your wedding	This is an offense guests won't forgive or forget. They won't be expecting to pay for anything, especially if they have spent hundreds of dollars on airfare to get to your event. If you can't provide a full bar, then offer beer, wine, champagne punch, and maybe one signature drink. Or invite fewer people, so you can throw a party worth attending.
Not including vegetarian choices in your menu	Your caterer will probably count on 10 percent of the guests being vegetarian, but you should make sure that you accommodate them. Incorporate vegetarian hors d'oeuvres into the menu as well. Find out about any of your guests' dietary restrictions (mom and mom-in-law can help) before you finalize your menu with the caterer.

ETIQUETTE DON'T	STRATEGY
Allowing toasts to become roasts	Remind your toastmasters to keep it brief (under two minutes) and to save inside jokes or bachelor-party antics for boys' night out. To muzzle a truly offensive roaster (who is turning your wedding into a train wreck), a predesignated relative can walk up and interrupt the speaker by applauding during a pause in the toast and then tactfully commandeer the mike.
Cranking the music when people are trying to talk	It's a wedding, not a U2 concert. Keep the music level loud enough for people to hear it, but not so loud that they feel they're in a downtown club. Talk to the band or DJ prior to the reception in order to set appropriate music levels.
***Ratatouille,* what's that? Serving exotic foods your guests can't identify**	While many of your guests will be thrilled to go ethnic, some will be put off. Save the exotic stuff for the appetizers and serve more familiar dishes as the main entrée.
Letting the reception drag on	Keep the festivities moving along (dinner, toasts, cake cutting, etc.) so those who want to leave after three or four hours don't feel like they'll be missing anything.
Being too concerned with perfection, and showing it	Don't worry about every little detail. Accept the fact that once the reception begins, it's too late to worry much about what might or might not happen. The more fun the bridal couple is having, the more fun everyone else will have.

Hip Tip. It's perfectly fine—and fun—to do things out of order. Have cocktails and appetizers first, then the ceremony, and then the rest of the party. People can mingle, you can take your time getting ready, and guests won't feel as if they are watching an opera production.

Hiring Vendors

Hiring the pros requires nerves of steel, lots of research, a clear head, the negotiating skills of Kissinger, and, ultimately, trust. The horror stories abound: food that never arrived or was substandard, flowers that wilted or were the wrong color, the DJ who came with a bubble machine but forgot to bring the right CDs. Just thinking about these unfortunate possibilities is enough to give you an anxiety attack before you make your first phone call. Here is a practical guide to hiring the best people for your dream day:

- **Keep your ear firmly to the ground.** Always use referrals from people you trust and check the grapevine for gossip.

- **Comparison shop.** For every vendor you need to hire, interview at least three candidates and get estimates. Before making a decision, weigh the pros and cons of hiring each person. And don't just go with the cheapest—there may be a reason for those low prices.

- **Do a background check.** This means checking with *recent* references, calling the Better Business Bureau, and running a Google search on the person's or company's name. If there's any bad press, you *will* find it.

- **Get it in writing.** In addition to reading and signing the vendor's standard contract, draw up a letter of agreement with all agreed-upon services, which both of you will sign. (If they don't have their own standard contract, consider yourself warned.)

- **Study the fine print.** Look for hidden costs, service charges, and taxes that will plump up your bill. If you find anything, call them on it. If they won't alter the contract, move on.

- **Have a lawyer look at the contract.** If you don't have a lawyer buddy to review it, then check out www.nolo.com (Nolo Press) for self-help legal advice.

OH, BEHAVE! Under no circumstances is there to be a "tip jar" anywhere near your reception. The coat check folks, bartenders, valet parking attendants, and other service providers who have direct contact with your guests should be made aware that tips will be covered by the hosts and that they should politely decline tips offered by guests.

Tips on Tipping

Most of us know the basics of tipping waiters, massage therapists, and hair-stylists, but when it comes to tipping wedding vendors, we may find ourselves in uncharted territory. Whom do you tip, and how much? Vendors on your tip list will probably include musicians, caterers, bartenders, waitstaff, parking attendants, coat check staff, makeup artists, and hairstylists, and possibly a limo driver. Here are some general rules to tip by:

- Tips are earned and should *never* be expected.

- Check your vendor's paperwork to see if they will include the gratuity in the final bill, a common practice with caterers and limo companies. If so, make sure you agree with the amount before paying.

- Tip in cash (or by check) after services have been rendered—this way, you can wait until services are performed before assessing how much to tip (or whether you want to tip at all).

- Appoint the best man, the wedding consultant, or a reliable pal the designated tipper.

- Prepare tips in advance. Put them in envelopes, seal them, and label them according to service or vendor, and then give them to your designated tip-per on the day of the wedding. Chances are that they'll do a fine job. If not, alert your designated tipper to any changes in the tip amount.

HOW TO KEEP IT *REAL SIMPLE* YET APPROPRIATE

Here's what Elizabeth Mayhew, editor of *Real Simple* magazine, has to say:

- **Renting is classy.** Rent wineglasses and white plates: clean, classic, beautiful.

- **Reusing something doesn't mean you're cheap.** Think about repurposing things like flower arrangements. For example, take the centerpiece made of lemons and lemon leaves from your rehearsal dinner, add white flowers, and place it on the head table at the reception.

- **Choose foods that can be eaten standing up.** For dessert, consider serving treats like cookies, cupcakes, and truffles. Says Elizabeth Mayhew, "Cupcakes are a favorite at *Real Simple*. They come in their own single-serving wrapper, and all you need is a napkin."

- **Serve cold dishes.** Salads, quiches, and roasted chicken can all be served at room temperature.

TIPPING CHEAT SHEET

So the waiter wasn't so great, but the coat check girl went beyond the call of duty. How much do you tip them? Use this chart as a guide. The basic tip is for standard services rendered, and the generous tip is for excellent service that was above your expectations.

Service Provider	Standard Tip	Generous Tip
Limousine driver*	15% of limo bill	20% of limo bill
Coat room and bathroom attendants	$1 per guest	$2 per guest
Bartender*	10% of total liquor bill	15% of total liquor bill
Makeup artist or hairstylist	15% of fee	20% of fee
DJ or band	$20 per DJ or musician	$25 per DJ or musician
Florist, photographer, or baker	None	Up to 15% for extra services only
Officiant	$100	$200 (if travel is involved)
Organist (ceremony)	Usually included in rental fee; if not, $50 for each performer	$75 for each performer
Valet parking attendant	$.50 per car	$1 per car
Waitstaff*	$10 per staff member	$20 per staff member
Caterer*	15% of food and drink bill	20% of food and drink bill

Check your contract to find out if gratuity is included in the final price. If so, there's no need to give any additional money.

Sticky Situations

A wedding reception is a fun and exciting event, but it can also seem like a complex behemoth. The unexpected will happen, despite your most careful planning. Review the following tricky situations to see how you might handle them.

Little Bobby is running loose at your reception and his parents are MIA.

Solution: Have your wedding consultant or maid of honor alert the parents to the fact that their child nearly toppled the cake. If this doesn't send ice water running through their veins, nothing will. If the parents are unavailable, try to get the child under control without making too much of a scene. The child is probably just overexcited and will go back to his or her designated table if gently reprimanded.

You're planning your two-hundred-guest reception from three thousand miles away.

Solution: Hire a wedding planner who operates in the city where the reception will be held. Fly out and meet her—she'll be your eyes and ears during the planning process. You'll also need to multitask with gusto. Every trip you make to the wedding city should be jam-packed with appointments with wedding vendors. You'll need to make decisions quickly, and you'll want to use all the help you can get. If some of your relatives or friends live in the wedding city, delegate tasks to anyone who offers.

OH, BEHAVE! If you're having a formal wedding, it's not in the best taste to hire a DJ in place of a band. Save the DJ for more informal settings or for the after-parties.

DIARY OF A CATERER, OR THE EVILS OF SKIMPING

According to Peg Devlin, a New York caterer, the biggest mistake brides make is to cut costs by "cheaping out" on the food, music, and labor—in her eyes, the most important aspects of a wedding reception. She describes one wedding that she considers the worst she's ever worked, held at the construction site of the couple's future home, right next to a cow field. Picture this: a bunch of uncomfortable guests standing in stifling heat, with no tent and no shade. There were two portapotties for 150 people, and two Weber grills to cook the forty pounds of lamb. The entertainment consisted of a stereo hooked up to a generator, and, unfortunately, the generator was so loud that nobody could hear the music. Guests were miserable, and when all was said and done this day was lodged in their memories for all the wrong reasons.

Peg says you can definitely do a low-budget celebration without sacrificing quality. All it takes is planning and a little creativity. One bride she knows "funked up" a barn Louisiana style—flowers and candles in mason jars on the tables, vintage lanterns hung from the rafters, mismatched gingham and period tablecloths, a few portable fire pits, an ice-filled clawfooted bathtub with beer and wine, and gumbo served as the main entrée, all accompanied by a live R&B band. The party ended up being inexpensive and was a great time for everyone.

One of your guests is dangerously drunk at the reception.

Solution: To keep the day as relaxed as possible, prepare for this possibility by developing a game plan. Caterer Catherine Kitz recommends having a designated family member enlist the help of the drunkard's spouse or date to keep him away from the bar and separate him from his car keys. The bride and groom should be spared from worrying about such unpleasant details. Also, meet with your bartender prior to W-day and give him a list of names and corresponding photos of friends and relatives who have a reputation for getting seriously loopy at gatherings; an experienced bartender will know how to be firm without being insulting. Encourage him to make drinks with a one-jigger limit.

You hate buffet-style meals but are having an informal wedding.

Solution: There's no requirement that you must have a buffet at an informal wedding. A great alternative is to do a family-style sit-down meal: large serving dishes of food are placed in the center of each table, and your guests help themselves to whatever they like. As a result, you won't make your guests stand in a long buffet line, and they won't have to dodge across the dance floor holding a flimsy plate. The number of servers is about the same as that for a buffet, but instead of scooping out servings, they bring the serving dishes to each table and clear the used dishes after each course.

Due to a last-minute scheduling conflict, you'll have a two-hour lag between ceremony and reception.

Solution: Two hours is a big chunk of time, and your guests shouldn't be forced to stand around waiting for the reception to start. We suggest setting up a cocktail hour, complete with hors d'oeuvres, at a nearby location (inform guests prior to the wedding date). If the cause of the snafu is an oversight by the reception hall, look into getting compensation for the additional food and drinks being served. If the snafu arises at the very last minute (the day of or the day before), then have your attendants get on the phone and find a nearby location that can accommodate everyone. Driving directions to the new spot can be handed out at the ceremony.

Hip Tip. *WeddingBells* magazine breaks the wedding magazine mold. Its user-friendly size and weight, fashion-forward approach, and contemporary editorial stance keep its content fresh, current, and believable. Check out their etiquette column to get ideas for solutions to vexing dilemmas. Visit www.weddingbells.com.

A vendor didn't come through with services promised.

Solution: Whether the DJ service sent someone you weren't expecting or the florist brought the wrong type of flowers, vendor mistakes can be infuriating. If you're unhappy because of the error, you need to take action (but this doesn't mean that you need to lose your cool). First, clearly but calmly communicate your dissatisfaction to the vendor, doing this either yourself or through your bridal consultant, and ask the vendor to reduce their bill. If that doesn't work, withhold final payment until you've come to an agreement with the vendor. Regardless, write an explicit yet professional letter to the company's owner clearly describing your experience dealing with them and report the problem company to the Better Business Bureau.

GUEST EXPECTATIONS, PART II

If you're familiar with proper guest behavior, you'll have a better idea of how to handle it if you're faced with someone's inappropriate behavior during the reception. Good guests do the following:

1. **Know that the bride wears the white.** Guests should avoid wearing anything that could remotely be perceived as competing with bridal attire.

2. **Dress appropriately.** If it's a formal wedding held at ten o'clock in the morning, they know not to wear that cleavage-bearing red velvet evening dress. A good guest would go with a classic, short, dressy ensemble. For a beach wedding, a vintage Lily Pulitzer sundress worn with a gardenia behind the ear would do nicely.

3. **Don't advertise their availability or show their predatory instincts.** The wedding guest hoping to score who wears the slinky black number with a plunging neckline is only to be pitied for her desperation and lack of decorum.

4. **Take care to go light on the booze.** They keep in mind that it's the most important day of the couple's lives. The last thing a bride needs is to have a sloppy guest teetering into in her expensive centerpiece or getting into a drunken Roe v. Wade argument with a right-wing relative during dinner.

5. **Engage in polite conversation:** Remember when your grandmother told you that it's never polite to discuss money, politics, or religion at the table? She had a point.

Your cousin, a professional caterer, has offered his services as a wedding gift to you, but you have misgivings.

Solution: A caterer (or any service provider, for that matter) can be expensive, so you'd stand to save quite a bit if you took your relative up on his offer. We recommend spending the money to hire someone not related to you. A relative's wedding gift of free professional services can turn out to be a cloud without a silver lining. Your cousin may not have the skills or experience to be able to create the sophisticated spread you want, and because he would be working for free, he might cut corners, not devote 100 percent to your event, or have a "you get what you get" attitude, since this is a freebie. And if he doesn't come through, what are you going to do? Not speak to him at your family Christmas party? Our advice: thank your cousin for his offer, but let him know that you want him to enjoy himself at your wedding. Tell him that if he were working the event he'd be so focused on the job that he wouldn't be able to have any fun, and that you really want all of your friends and relatives to be free to celebrate with you. Then hire someone based on reputation and skills and spend the money, so you can rest assured that you'll get what you want.

Your photographer is very disruptive at your rehearsal dinner, and you're afraid of what might happen at the wedding.

Solution: An overly chatty or intrusive photographer who gets in the way instead of capturing the moment can create stress for the couple and their guests, which is a definite etiquette violation. On the morning before the wedding, ask your wedding consultant or a designated point person to have a talk with him, suggesting in a friendly way that he try to capture the moment without killing it, offering an example of how to better handle a specific situation. Making a tactful, well-placed comment will go far in controlling most vendors—after all, they want to be paid, and most want to do a good job.

CHAPTER 10

THE RECEIVING END—Gifts

The wedding gift is a sticky subject for us gals—we don't want to appear as if we are in it for the goods, yet we secretly fantasize about outfitting the perfect crib (just think, here's your chance to finally get a set of Frette sheets or Le Creuset cookware). We're not supposed to expect gifts, but we know that guests will give us gifts. So how do we conduct ourselves with decorum, appearing gracious and nonmaterialistic, and still get what we want? You'll find the answers in this chapter, which covers the etiquette of gift giving (to our attendants, family, and fiancé), gift getting, and expressing thanks, and offers some examples of tricky gift-related situations and how to manage them.

The Golden Rules

Gifts for the Couple: THE TRADITION

There are etiquette rules associated with gift giving and receiving that can create some seriously awkward situations. One rule—the main rule, in fact—that causes quite a bit of bridal confusion is the following: Brides and grooms should not expect a gift, and hence should never ask for a particular gift. Sounds simple enough, right? It gets trickier. Because we know most guests will buy a gift and because we know that they'll want to give us something we'll enjoy, we're expected to make things easier on them. It is with delicate discretion, then, that the bride makes her guests' gift-selection process as painless as possible by gently steering them toward items she desires—via the gift registry. *But the situation gets even more confusing:* the bride is not supposed to discuss that same gift registry that she so painstakingly created. Now, guests know that they should buy a gift, but they also know that the bride isn't supposed to expect a gift or discuss gifts at all, so they must discreetly ask her parents or attendants about where she's registered.

If this all sounds like a lot of pussyfooting around a social convention, it is. Unfortunately, this is how it's been done for centuries. And, Anti-Bride or not, you need to do it this way, too. It is just fine to have your maid of honor discreetly get the word out for you. But you can't send out a blanket e-mail to your guests in an effort to commandeer the goods.

Time Capsule. The bridal registry was born in the 1800s when a French silverware manufacturer, who understood the communication and travel constraints of the time, came up with the idea. Since parents seemed to know best back then, it was they and not the bride who set up the master gift list. It shaved weeks off the guests' sleuthing process and saved the bride countless hours of waiting in line to return that extra butter churn or cast-iron skillet.

In days past, wedding gifts were meant to help the newly married couple set up their new home. Most newlyweds were young (late teens and early twenties) and just starting out, and they didn't already have complete sets of dishes, linens, sheets, towels, appliances, and decorative items, so these gifts were integral to their new life together. The practicality of those wedding gifts led to the development of two gift-giving rules. The first rule is that they should give the couple a gift within a year after the wedding (so they can use it in their new home). The second (but lesser known) rule is that they shouldn't show up at the nuptials with a box under their arm—they should send it, ideally before the wedding, instead. The frequency with which people ignore this rule is high on our list of annoyances. Pressing the bride and groom into sherpa duty on their wedding night? *Perish the thought!* But why does this rule persist? Imagine, it's your wedding: you're dancing, mingling, toasting, and then, the getaway. *But not so fast*—first you have to deal with four carloads of boxes of various sizes, many with fragile contents (another microwave or DVD player?) before you can finally escape to your honeymoon suite. It winds up being more moving day than getaway, and a sure wedding-night passion killer. Of course, the sherpa duties don't always fall to the happy couple. They're often left to an already exhausted or inebriated member of the wedding party and/or the couples' parents. Even the most conscientious attendant can't prevent broken crystal or retrieve a misplaced gift card. The rule of thumb: To save everyone unnecessary trouble, send it in advance, then have a cocktail and dance!

Time Capsule. In Victorian times most wedding gifts were sent well in advance and were displayed at the reception if, and only if, the reception was held at the home of the bride's parents.

OH, BEHAVE!
According to tradition, if you elope, you shouldn't register for gifts. Etiquette gurus will tell you that you've excluded your friends and family from your special day and so they shouldn't feel obligated to buy gifts. If a reception is held after the couple returns home, gifting is perfectly appropriate (but still should not be expected by the couple).

HOW TO SET UP A FAT-FREE, GUILT-FREE REGISTRY THAT'S KIND TO YOUR GUESTS

1. **Shop with the big boys.** Go with stores like Macy's, Williams-Sonoma, Pottery Barn, Crate & Barrel, and Target, where return policies are flexible and you can return things by mail in almost any state.

2. **Keep it practical.** Form really does follow function. Pick items that will stand the test of time: high-quality cookware, dinnerware, knives, bedding, towels, outdoor and camping equipment, and home accents.

3. **Don't do a color theme.** It's too difficult for your friends and family to find items in a specific color. Stick to basics: look for products made of chrome, silver or silver plate, stainless steel, white or black enamel or durable plastic, sparkling white china, crystal, glass, and beautiful white bedding and towels.

4. **Register for a variety of gifts in a wide price range.** Remember, not everyone can afford a $200 gold-plated picture frame. Choose modestly priced items that your fiscally challenged pals can handle: wineglasses, kitchen gadgets, placemats, and kitchen towels.

5. **Make your lifestyle obvious.** This way, guests can deviate a bit from your registry but keep to a general theme you've created. If you and your mate entertain outdoors, register for a well-made grill and utensils at Williams-Sonoma, or camping equipment at REI. Then, guests who want to choose nonregistry gifts will know to look for other barbecue or camping items.

6. **Respect people's decision not to buy from your registry.** If a guest gives you something nonreturnable that you just can't use, remember that it's the thought that counts. You may be able to give it to someone else or sell it on eBay or at a garage sale. Better yet, keep it in a cabinet and then bring it out when the loved one comes for a visit.

Gifts for the Wedding Party: THE TRADITION

It's hard to put a price tag on the many things your friends and family have done for you in the months leading up to the big day, so finding that perfect thank-you gift can sometimes be a challenge. Those on your gift list should include attendants (including flower girls, ring bearers, and junior bridesmaids), parents, and other helpers such as readers and flower arrangers. There are ways around spending big bucks on these gifts—the rule of thumb is to keep it thoughtful. A photo of you and your friend set in a sterling frame is more personal and meaningful than cubic zirconium stud earrings.

Many brides will give their bridesmaids something gorgeous to wear on the big day to unify their look: a sparkly necklace, earrings, purse, or cashmere shawl. Gifts for parents might include engraved cuff links, custom-designed earrings, a day at a spa, tickets to the opera, or dinner for two. For other helpers, bottles of private-label wine shipped from a boutique vineyard in a gift box would fill the bill nicely. Buy something you would want, and then give it, keeping in mind the tastes of your attendants, of course.

Giving Thanks: THE TRADITION

Wedding gifts range from wonderfully thoughtful and generous to unoriginal and downright hideous. When you receive a gift that falls in the latter category, don't insult your guest with a simple "Thanks for the gift, signed Jane." You should muster up enough creativity to let the person know you truly appreciate their gesture (even if you don't love their gift). Here are some hints to help you along.

THANK-YOU NOTE MAGIC FORMULA

1. Thank them for sharing the day with you or, if they weren't able to come to the wedding, thank them for thinking of you.

2. Thank them for the gift and describe it with some detail (using a positive adjective and some identifying detail).

3. Tell them how you plan to use it.

4. Reiterate your thanks and tell them that you look forward to seeing them (at your wedding), that it was great seeing them (at your wedding), or that you look forward to seeing them (after you return from your honeymoon).

5. Sign off with words like "with thanks," "much love," "warmly," or "yours."

THANK-YOU NOTE EXAMPLES

Thanks for money:

Dear Aunt Millie,

It was wonderful seeing you at the wedding. Thank you so much for the generous wedding gift. Kevin and I are putting it toward a new home—thanks to you, we've almost got the down payment! We'll be driving down to see you soon.

Much love,
[Your names]

Thanks for a gift you dislike:

Dear Aunt Millie,

It was wonderful seeing you at the wedding. Kevin and I would like to thank you for the beautiful gold-plated elephant bookends. We're already using them to hold our new set of cookbooks we got at our bridal shower. Thank you again for coming to the wedding and sharing our special day.

Love,
[Your names]

Gift from group:

Dear Jane, Bill, and Mark,

It was wonderful seeing you at the wedding. Thank you for the beautiful place setting. Now we have service for six—just the right number to have you over for dinner! Can't wait to see you all again—let's plan something for next month. Talk to you soon.

Love,
[Your names]

You'll notice that graciousness and gratitude set the tone of these notes, whether or not the gift is liked.

DOS AND DONT'S OF THANK-YOU NOTES

- **Do send notes early.** For gifts received before the wedding, send a thank-you note right away—definitely within two weeks. After the wedding, send a note within a month, the sooner the better.

- **Don't send preprinted messages or typed or e-mailed thank-you's.** It's not only tacky but also unappreciative. Send a handwritten note on nice note cards.

- **Do keep careful records.** When something arrives, jot down what the gift is and who sent it. You'll respect yourself in the morning.

- **Do enlist your partner.** Don't take on the entire burden yourself. Come up with a plan for getting all of the notes done—maybe you could each write five notes every morning until they're done, or take an afternoon on the weekend and bang them all out.

- **Do keep it thoughtful.** Visualize using the gift (if it's a set of red table linens, think of using them at Christmas dinner) and put your thoughts on paper. The time you took to thank the giver will be greatly appreciated.

New Rules of the Road

Gifts run the gamut from a new set of All-Clad to snorkling in Bali. To get in front of getting what you really want and avoid spending precious newlywed time waiting in the return line at Macy's, follow us as we show you how to rein in retail issues and get the goods without burning bridges.

Gifts for the Couple: FORGING YOUR OWN PATH

Today, the majority of couples marry later than they did in the past, often live together first, and typically have at least one of everything. So what's left to acquire? According to Carolyn, they should shoot for items they long for—a professional-grade digital camera or high-end backpacking gear. In her case, a Le Corbusier leather chaise longue was the ticket. When guests asked, her mother gave them the option of the registry at the groovy furniture store (along with other options, such as Borders and Williams-Sonoma) where they could contribute any amount toward the chaise and have a gift card sent to the couple. The result: the couple got a great piece of furniture that they loved and had ten fewer salad spinners to return.

VIRTUAL BRIDE

The Internet has opened many new doors for both guests and brides-to-be. Guests can buy and send wedding gifts, and brides no longer have to go in person to multiple department stores to set up registries—it's as simple as pointing and clicking. The best part: no more spending a perfectly sunny Saturday in a crowded department store zapping merchandise with a SKU gun along with a host of other bedraggled betrothed. Using Web registries, you can easily take control of your hope chest and even give it some international flair: Get your cookware from Paris, your bath towels from New York, your wine from Italy. Enlist your maid of honor to relay information and links.

HONEYMOON REGISTRIES

Do you long to take a cooking class while honeymooning in Provence? Go spear fishing with your new husband in Bali? How about a taking a horseback-riding lesson in Australia? Trip registries are all the rage, says Nancy Bodace, owner of www.HoneyLuna.com, one of the first wedding registry Web sites for honeymoons. "We create a gift registry for couples that contains fun things they can do on their honeymoon, which people can buy as their wedding gift. It's just like the registry you'd find in the store." Guests can put money toward your airfare, pay for a night at that funky waterfront bungalow, or buy you a romantic dinner for two. You create a custom registry with activities tailored to your individual lifestyle, including much-needed post-wedding massages for two.

Stress Saver. Don't be pressured into giving your fiancé a wedding gift (or expect a wedding gift from him). We think this development is yet another diamond-industry scheme to get you to consume more. If you prefer, agree to give yourselves, as a couple, new furniture or an extra week of your honeymoon. Or save the money for a down payment on fabulous new digs.

Sticky Situations

Giving and receiving gifts graciously is easy for some people but difficult for others. Here's what to do if you find yourself with a gift-related dilemma.

You'd like to receive money instead of traditional gifts.

Solution: Because it's never okay to ask for money, the key is discretion. To indirectly get the word out, rely on the family grapevine. One bride's mother, who was contacted by guests about gift registries, provided them with the names of stores where the couple had registered but also subtly suggested that if they wanted to do something easy they could contribute to the couple's "down payment fund" for their future house. Another bride's mother suggested to guests that they buy gift certificates from stores like Williams-Sonoma, Borders, Macy's, and Home Depot. Guests still felt like they were giving a gift, and the couple bought items they really needed.

THE PSYCHOLOGICAL IMPACT OF GIFT GIVING (OR NOT)

Consider this: You've returned from your gloriously relaxing honeymoon and sit down to open your wedding gifts. As you write down the gifts and the names of the senders, you notice that your best friend's name doesn't appear on the list. "Oh well," you think, "she's probably just having a hard time deciding what to give us; surely she'll give us something soon." But months go by and it soon becomes clear that she decided not to give you a wedding gift. Ouch!

Etiquette experts say that stressing over whether or not you get wedding gifts from certain people is materialistic, and they advise brides to let it go. But brides are singing a different tune. Every one we've talked to says that it's not about the goods; it's the thought (or lack thereof) that hurts the most. Ask any bride, and she'll tell you that she couldn't help making a mental note of who gave and who didn't. One bride, Kristin, who had been the maid of honor at a college friend's wedding, bought a set of vintage Russell Wright dinnerware for the couple (they collected it). Unfortunately, when Kristin got married, her friend did not reciprocate. To this day, she feels that it compromised their relationship. Petty? We think not.

Etiquette expert Syndie Seid says that under no circumstances can you ask someone why they didn't give you a gift, even if it's your best friend. It would be tantamount to fishing for compliments—once you sink your hook, even the most heartfelt praise will mean much less. She recommends sending a note thanking the friend for their presence at the wedding, which just might compel him or her to send you a little token. If your friend still doesn't get it, then move on—it's not worth the fight.

A gift arrives broken or damaged.

Solution: If the gift was sent directly by the retailer where it was bought, you're in luck. Just contact the retailer and see about getting a replacement or credit toward other merchandise. There's no need for you or the store to involve the giver at all. If the gift was mailed by the giver, then check the box to see if it has an insurance stamp. If it does, send it back to the giver with an apologetic explanatory note so she can get reimbursement from the post office and (possibly) send you a replacement. If there is no stamp, you may still want to break the news to her (she might wonder where those Waterford crystal candlesticks are if she ever comes to visit). She may still have the receipt and be willing to give it to you or to deal with the retailer herself. Make sure she knows that you do not expect a replacement gift.

You get a gift from someone you don't intend to invite.

Solution: You're not obligated to invite him or her. Send the person a warm note of thanks and leave it at that.

Your wedding is canceled.

Solution: There's only one thing to do in this case, and that is to send every gift back, even monogrammed gifts. Send them with a handwritten note telling them that the wedding has been canceled and letting them know you appreciate their gift. Don't worry about giving them a reason for the cancellation—they don't need one.

You've gotten duplicate gifts and you'd like to return them, but you know it's in poor taste to ask the giver where they bought them.

Solution: If we're talking about sheets, towels, or other daily-use items, keep them—you'll use them eventually. If we're talking about two vacuum cleaners or other items that you simply can't use two of, then see if the person closest to the relative (your mother, perhaps) feels comfortable enough with the person to let them know what happened and find out where it was purchased.

OH, BEHAVE! To e-mail guests with your gift registry information, to include your registry in anything you send to guests (your invitations, maps and directions, or list of nearby hotels), or to mention it on your wedding Web site is considered to be in bad form.